BBC Books, an imprint of Ebury Publishing
20 Vauxhall Bridge Road, London SW1V 2SA
BBC Books is part of the Penguin Random House group of companies
whose addresses can be found at global.penguinrandomhouse.com

Penguin
Random House
UK

This book is published to accompany the television series Strictly Come Dancing first broadcast
on BBC One in 2022.

Executive Producer: Sarah James
Series Director: Nikki Parsons
Series Producer: Jack Gledhill

With thanks to: Harriet Frost, Eve Winstanley, Joe Turner, Stefania Aleksander, Phoebe Grief, Kate Lawson,
Kim Winston, Jack Gledhill, Fiona Pearce and Victoria Dalton.

First published by BBC Books in 2022
www.penguin.co.uk

A CIP catalogue record for this book is available from the British Library.

ISBN 9781785948084

Printed and bound in Italy by Elcograf S.p.A

Picture credits: © BBC Archive. BBC/Ray Burmiston: pp. 6, 10, 12, 22, 24, 30, 32, 36, 38,
40, 44, 46, 48, 50, 52, 56, 58, 64, 66, 68, 70, 72, 78, 80, 82, 84, 86, 92, 94, 98, 100, 102, 104,
106, 108, 110, 112, 114, 116, 118, 120, 122, 124.
BBC/Guy Levy: pp. 9, 14–21, 35, 89–91
Dave Hogan: pp. 26, 29
Seamus Ryan: p28

ANNUAL

BOOKS

Contents

Meet the Pro Dancers

Strictly Features

Fun and Trivia

Shirley Ballas

Head judge Shirley is keen to welcome the series-20 celebrities to the dance floor and is thrilled with the latest recruits. As always, the Queen of Latin will be watching the couples closely, encouraging them from the sidelines and offering sound advice.

'My job is to keep an open mind for all 15 celebrities, so I'm doing that,' she says. 'I'll be looking at the quality of how they move, how they interact with their pro and what unique attributes they bring to the show.

'But I think the 2022 cast are outstanding and everybody's in for a real treat yet again. Each year, the team find a great range of celebrities. They never cease to amaze me.'

As the new series gets off to a sparkling start, Shirley can't wait for the many highlights ahead.

'I'm excited about returning to Blackpool, but also about Movie Week, Halloween Week and Musicals Week,' she says. 'I'm excited about not having any partitions between Anton, Motsi and me, so if I want to have a little dance with Motsi or to show a ballroom frame with Anton, I can. And I think my arm can stretch across and give Craig a little tap on the shoulder if he's out of order!'

Shirley is pleased to see Anton back in the judge's chair and says he proved the 'perfect fit' on the panel last year.

'I've known Anton for 30 years and I love sitting next to him. He's done absolutely brilliantly as a judge and fitted in like a sock in a shoe. I have a bucket-list dream to dance a Foxtrot with Anton on the show at some point, so watch this space.'

As a former Latin champ, with a 40-year career in both competing and teaching, Shirley is offering a warm welcome to the four new professionals – Vito Coppola, Carlos Gu, Lauren Oakley and Michelle Tsiakkas.

'We have 20 professionals this year, to celebrate 20 years of *Strictly*, and I can tell you these professionals are outstanding. Our team scours the world to find great dancers, and they certainly have done that. It's lovely to see boys and girls get onto a show which has been their dream and that they've been watching since childhood. We're delighted to have them on board.'

Shirley says last year's Final – between Rose Ayling-Ellis and John Whaite – was unforgettable, but the highlight of the series was Rose and Giovanni's Couple's Choice dance.

'The stand-out moment was when the music stopped during the dance, because no one was expecting that,' she says. 'Rose kept the rhythm and showed us into her world. She captured the hearts of the nation and inspired us to dream big. She should be very proud of that.'

The new series promises more thrills and spills and Shirley says that *Strictly* is the gift that keeps on giving.

'We have a great line-up, the best professionals in the world, and we're led by the A-team, who are mind-blowing, from Executive Producer Sarah James down. For us judges, as well as the viewers, there's always something unique and special that gets us excited. So hold on to your hats, because *Strictly* is back.'

Winner's Story
Rose Ayling-Ellis

In ten silent seconds, when the music stopped and Rose Ayling-Ellis danced on, she and partner Giovanni Pernice created one of *Strictly*'s most iconic moments – and stole the heart of the nation. The pair went on to recreate their Couple's Choice in the Final, leaving viewers in tears and ultimately winning the *Strictly* crown.

The *EastEnders* star, who has been deaf since birth, says her powerful week-eight performance had a huge impact that spread way beyond the deaf community.

'The reaction was crazy,' she says. 'The Couple's Choice is such a specialist dance and Gio really put in the work to get it right. When Giovanni first presented me with the silent idea, I said, "Let's go for it." We thought it'd be a good chance to show the audience, briefly, what it's like to be deaf, but we didn't think it would have that much impact. I think people loved it because we made it a joyful thing. It's not sad or depressing. We showed it's okay to hear the silence. It can be beautiful.'

Rose was inundated with hundreds of messages after the dance, with many people from the deaf community saying she had inspired them.

'A lot of people said they had started to become more confident and able to accept they are different,' she says. 'I am super-proud that I have had that impact.' Their dance also won the Must-See Moment award at the BAFTAs, the only award voted for by the public, showing how it had inspired viewers across the country.

As the first deaf contestant in the UK, she wanted to 'challenge the stereotype' and prove that deaf people can move to music.

'The first week I was really surprised by how intense the training was,' she says. 'But the journey has been incredible. I didn't think I would get to the Final, let alone win.

'But in my week-five Viennese Waltz, when I began to put my acting into the dance, I realised I might be able to go to the next level.'

The Viennese Waltz earned Rose a score of 37, including her first 10, from Shirley Ballas. The following week she bagged the first 40 of the series for her brilliant Tango, to Ed Sheeran's 'Shivers', and she continued to wow every week until the Final.

'When I watched the series back from beginning to end, I could finally see how much I'd improved,' she says. 'It's only then you realise how much you process.'

As well as the Couple's Choice, Rose and Giovanni repeated their *Frozen*-themed Quickstep in the Final and performed a stunning showdance to 'The Rose' by Bette Midler – earning a total score of 119 out of a possible 120.

It was a close call, with fellow finalists John Whaite and Johannes Radebe matching their score, but the public vote handed the glitterball to Rose.

'I just couldn't believe I made it all the way. I didn't want it to end. If you asked me to do another ten weeks, I would do it!'

Rose says being crowned *Strictly* champion is a moment she'll never forget.

'I was speechless,' she says. 'After the very last dance, Giovanni and I got really emotional, and I was crying so much I had to redo my make-up to

go back onstage. But when I won, I didn't cry. I felt like I'd come out of my own body. It was only when I hugged my mum afterwards that I burst into tears.'

Rose's performances on the show also helped to promote the use of British Sign Language (BSL) and all the pros, including Giovanni, made an effort to learn some signing.

'Gio's naturally got it in him because he's very expressive,' Rose says. 'When he met my deaf friends, they tested him out, getting him to sign to them, and he didn't do badly.'

The Kent-born actress credits Giovanni with much of her success on the show and says he's a 'very good teacher'.

'Gio's very strict, but he really wants to get the best out of you and he never gives up,' she says. 'He believed in me more than I believe in myself sometimes. I have learned so much about myself. Gio is now a friend for life, and it has been a very special journey for me.'

Since the show, Rose has performed in the Live Tour and won an Inspirational Person of the Year award at the Visionary Honours, as well as picking up an Unmissable TV Moment of the Year gong, with Giovanni, for the Couple's Choice dance.

'The impact of me taking part in *Strictly* has been beyond my wildest expectations and it's amazing. I can't believe how much my life has changed in such a short amount of time.'

Helen
Skelton

Action girl Helen Skelton is no stranger to a challenge, having previously become the second woman to run the Namibian ultra-marathon, walked a tightrope between the chimneys of Battersea Power Station for Comic Relief and become the first person to reach the South Pole using a bicycle for Sport Relief.

She has also kayaked the full length of the Amazon River, breaking two Guinness World Records for the longest solo journey and the longest distance in a kayak in 24 hours by a woman. Now she says she's 'giddy with excitement' after taking on *Strictly* and her dance partner Gorka Márquez will be buoyed by her energy.

The TV and radio presenter started her career on *Newsround* before fronting *Blue Peter* for five years, from 2008. While there, she took part in Helen's Magnificent 7, taking on challenges set by Comic Relief including flying with the Red Arrows, crossing a rope bridge and breaking the then-World Record for the longest ever bunting. She went on to host *Countryfile* and coverage of the 2016 Olympics, as well as a regular Sunday show on BBC Radio 5 Live.

As a pupil, Helen welcomes being partnered with Gorka and says her intrepid past will help her in the training room.

'When I was on *Blue Peter*, I'd be told, "Tomorrow you're going to learn to be a rock climber," and then I'd be thrust onto a rock for 12 hours, or, "Tomorrow you're going to swim the Channel," so I'm used to life being quite intense and extreme. Gorka is absolutely ace and I'm really up for training to learn a new skill. I'll be very happy to put in the hours that I need to.'

Helen, a mum to two boys and a baby girl, says her family is over the moon that she'll be competing in the show this year.

'My family's really excited,' she says. 'I think this show, more than any other, is great for families. My mum is so excited and loves telling her friends that I'm doing *Strictly*.'

While she is keen to add another huge achievement to her long list by taking home the glitterball, Helen, who was born and raised in Cumbria, has another benchmark to aim for first.

'I just want to take it one week at a time,' she says. 'I know everyone always says, "I want to get to Blackpool," but all my family are in the north-west so I really do want to get to Blackpool. That would be a win for me.'

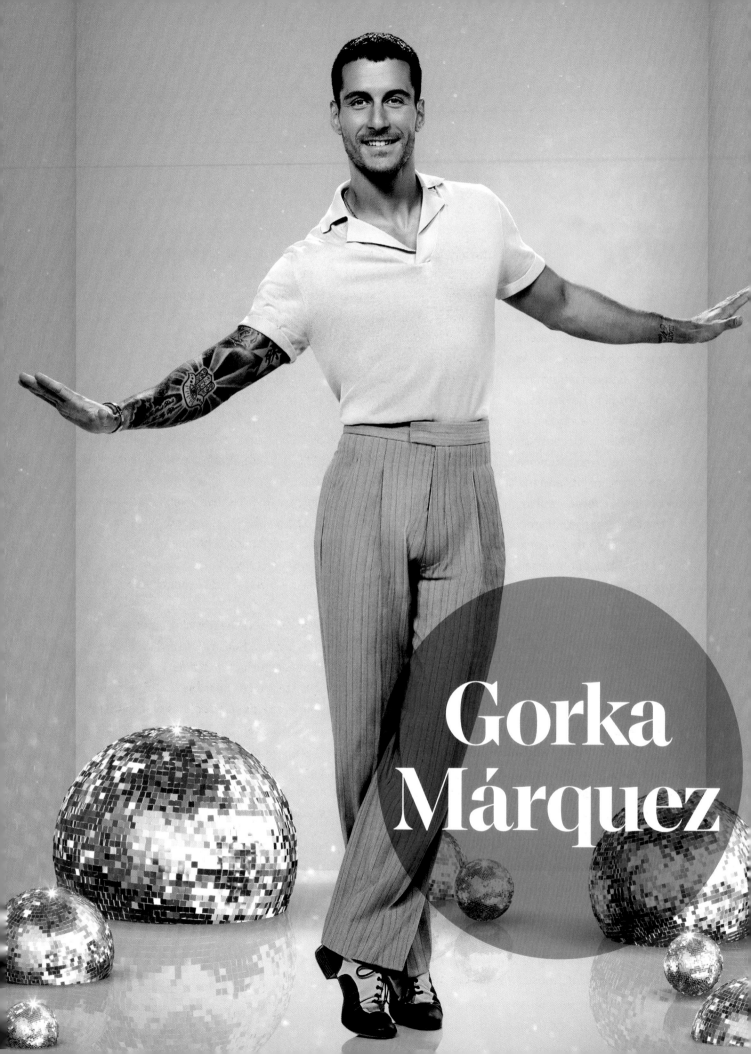

Gorka Márquez

Paired with intrepid presenter Helen Skelton, Gorka Márquez is conjuring up ways to channel her fearlessness into some adventurous routines. He reckons the former *Blue Peter* presenter, who has kayaked up the Amazon, reached the South Pole on a bicycle and run ultra-marathons in Africa, will take on everything he throws at her.

'I think Helen's bravery is a very positive thing for our partnership, because she is used to doing challenges and being thrown in at the deep end so she's not scared of lifts and tricks,' he says. 'When it comes to me choreographing, I know I don't have to worry that she's scared of the heights or of jumps, and she will throw herself into it.

'On the first day of rehearsal, I turned around and she was doing cartwheels, which is a great sign. She is physically fit and I think she has a great stamina – although I'll let you know when we do the Jive!'

Gorka has high hopes for Helen's dancing skills and was impressed with her in the opening group number.

'Helen has potential,' he says. 'She has coordination and rhythm, and in day one of training, she learned the steps and timing for half of the routine, which, in the first day of her *Strictly* journey, was very impressive.'

With an American Smooth as their first dance, Gorka has given his new partner some show-stopping lifts from the off and says she is bubbling with energy. But slowing her down may be his biggest challenge.

'Helen is so energetic. She's always moving and her approach to everything is "Let's do it." So I think for her, going into those slow dances may be challenging. I know she thinks she will be better with the fast ones. Also, she's very giggly so when I pull my serious face, she can't stop laughing, which could be an issue in a Paso Doble or Tango!'

Born in Bilbao, Spain, Gorka has been dancing since he was 11, representing his country in the World Latin Championships in 2010 and the semi-finals of the 2012 WDSF (World DanceSport Federation) World Cup. Since joining *Strictly* in 2016, he has twice made the Final, with Alexandra Burke and Maisie Smith, and last year he partnered soap star Katie McGlynn.

'Katie was great and we have a very similar sense of humour,' he says. 'She was a good student but because of a heavy filming schedule on *Hollyoaks*, she didn't have much time to train. But she was amazing and lovely and I had so much fun working with her.'

As a teacher, Gorka describes himself as 'disciplined, not strict', but says Helen's 'get-it-done' attitude is a perfect match for his.

'I like to get as much as possible done. In Helen's case, she has three kids so I don't want to keep her in the studio any longer than I have to. We will have plenty of laughs, but at the same time I want to get the job done.'

Going into the new series, Gorka is looking forward to taking northerner Helen to Blackpool and to creating great routines every week.

'With Helen, I see a lot of potential and things that make her a strong contestant, so I'm looking forward to dancing with her each week and making it as far as possible,' he says. 'It's my seventh series and seven is a lucky number, so hopefully that's a good omen and we can win the glitterball.'

Dance Class: Latin

Every dance has its own story, derived from diverse cultures around the globe, and of course every style has different steps and techniques.

In our very own dance class, we learn the origins of each dance, and *Strictly*'s Creative Director Jason Gilkison talks us through what the judges are looking for when each couple takes to the floor.

From the slow, sensual Rumba to the cheeky Cha-cha-cha, the Latin dances provide variety, drama and entertainment in spades.

Cha-cha-cha

The Cha-cha-cha, often shortened to the Cha-cha, originated in Cuba and evolved from the faster dance, the Mambo, popular in the 1940s jazz boom. Some couples struggled with the speed of the Mambo so the orchestras slowed the pace down. The new rhythm inspired dancers to add a hip syncopation to the forward and back breaks of a Mambo, which later evolved into a triple step.

Cuban violinist Enrique Jorrin, who composed the first Cha-cha song in 1948, named it after the shuffling sound the dancers' shoes made on the floor. The fun, flirty dance was introduced to the UK by dance teacher Pierre Lavelle after a visit to Cuba in 1952.

Jason says: 'For the Cha-cha, the judges are looking for a sharp, staccato action with the feet, but at the same time a soft action within the body. It's quite a difficult movement for the celebs to master because what the feet and body are doing is almost contradictory.

'The characterisation of the Cha-cha is also important. It's a light, fluffy, flirty, cheeky dance – not what I would call a sensual dance. If the Cha-cha could be a time of the day, it would be a Sunday afternoon.'

Samba

The Mardi Gras dance was made popular by the carnivals of Rio de Janeiro in the early twentieth century. An expression of pure joy, Samba has its roots in Africa and Brazil in the late nineteenth century, and the music and the dance spread through the streets of Rio and eventually into the general population, becoming part of the mainstream Latin dance scene in the 1930s.

Rumba

The sensual dance of love and seduction, the Rumba is sometimes called the grandfather of Latin dance. Like the Samba, it can also be traced back to African tribal dance, becoming a staple in the clubs of Havana in the later nineteenth century, and it remains a popular dance in Cuba today.

Jason says: 'Timing, timing, timing! Samba is all about the rhythm, the bounce and the timing. The more traditional steps, earlier than the 1960s, have a bounce action section and the more recent, faster steps don't, so you've got to be really clear where the bounce action comes in. The Samba rolls are tricky, because they're about two bodies almost moving as one. Then there's the timing of the knee, which is doing one thing, and the timing of the feet, which are doing something completely different. You've almost got to turn into a percussive instrument yourself to dance a good Samba.'

Jason says: 'The Rumba is known as a sexy, sensual dance, but to me it is one of the most beautiful dances if you get it right. Because of the nature of the straight legs, it can look quite stiff and, of course, the slower the dance, the more exposing it is, because it's difficult to cover anything up. Timing is key. The hold on the four, over two beats, is really important to get right. It's often quite a dangerous dance for the male or leading celebrity, because they look like they're not doing much, but they're doing a lot because they have to lead everything.'

Jive

Jason says: 'You have to remember that Jive is one of the Latin dances, so while you want very light legs and kicks and flicks, it is also a rhythmic dance. It has to keep that Latin feel. The partnering skills are really important, because it's the fastest of the Latin American dances, so the lead has to be intensely good. But you want it to be light, you want to be on the front part of your foot and you don't want your weight to go back, otherwise your Jive will be heavy. The temptation is to wear trainers or baseball shoes, but actually a higher shoe helps in getting a little bit of your weight forward.'

It's fast, furious and fun, and anyone attempting the Jive has to be fit as a fiddle to pull it off. Popularised in the 1930s by the publication of a dictionary by jazz musician Cab Calloway, the dance itself is based on the US swing style, which came over to the UK with the GIs in the Second World War in the form of the Lindy Hop and Jitterbug. British dancers soon adopted the term Jive for the faster, freer version.

Dance Class: Latin

Paso Doble

The most dramatic of the dances, the Paso Doble, which literally translates as 'two steps', is believed to have roots in both Spain and the South of France, and it tells the story of a bullfight. The leading partner represents the toreador, and the other dancer, most commonly, the cape, although occasionally it can be the bull or a second matador. The dance gained notoriety in Parisian high society in the 1930s, and many of the steps have French names.

Jason says: 'The leading person has to be the centre of that dance. The body weight is very high, almost up at the chest, and strong shapes are essential at all times. It's all about shape. You have to really imagine that the traditionally female role is becoming the cape and the male role is being the matador.'

Dance Class:
Ballroom

From the Hollywood glamour of the American Smooth to the whirlwind Viennese Waltz, the ballroom dances have something for everyone.

Foxtrot

The Foxtrot was introduced to the masses by legendary dancers Vernon and Irene Castle in 1914. Their inspiration, they said, was a dance performed at a private club for African Americans. The name Foxtrot is thought to have originated from a trotting dance performed by the vaudeville entertainer Harry Fox. The Foxtrot is a smooth dance with long walking movements and a combination of slow and quick steps, typically in the pattern slow-quick-quick or slow-slow-quick-quick.

Jason says: 'Foxtrot is the Rolls-Royce of all the ballroom dances, and you have to glide across that floor like a hot knife through butter. It's really important that you roll from foot to foot. Of all the ballroom dances it's the most exposing because you can see any bumps or jerks in this dance. You have to be together as one as you move across the floor.'

Viennese Waltz

The precursor to the English Waltz, the Viennese Waltz is the oldest of the ballroom dances; it first emerged in Europe in the mid-sixteenth century, being mentioned in print as early as 1580, and developed in the eighteenth century from a German dance called the Volta and an Austrian folk dance, the Ländler. It was the first closed-couple dance introduced into polite society where previously dances had been performed in a communal sequence, with individual dancers and couples facing outwards to spectators as much as inwards. To many, the closeness of the dancing was shocking, with one writer referring to it as 'godless' and another condemning it as the 'shameless, indecent whirling-dance'.

American Smooth

Think Fred Astaire and Ginger Rogers, and all the glamour of the Hollywood movies of the 1930s and 1940s. The American Smooth is based on the four ballroom disciplines of Foxtrot, Waltz, Tango and Viennese Waltz,

Waltz

The Waltz used in ballroom today is known as the English Waltz or Slow Waltz, danced at approximately 90 beats per minute with three beats to the bar, while the Viennese Waltz, considered the original dance, is around 180 beats per minute. As the Waltz spread across the globe, regional variations developed, particularly in the US and UK, with the slower tempo emerging in the late-nineteenth and early-twentieth centuries.

but it allows more time out of hold – up to 60 per cent of the dance – and more theatrical lifts. It was brought into the world of competitive dancing by legendary teacher Arthur Murray.

Jason says: 'The Waltz is usually the first dance that people learn and it's actually quite a tricky dance, because there is a lot of rotation. You have to make sure that, while you have the softness and the slowness, you also have the rotation. Swing and sway – that big pendulum action – is really important.'

Jason says: 'The American Smooth is based on classic ballroom dances, and the open work – out of hold – has to transport us to the 1940s. We have really to imagine that we're in a Fred and Ginger musical. Lifts are really important and they have to look effortless. You should not see where the lift begins or ends because it's so smoothly integrated into the dance.'

Ballroom Tango

The Tango is derived from the Argentine version, which hails from the streets of Buenos Aires. As the dance spread to New York and then Paris and London, through the Argentinian community, in the 1910s, the hold became slightly less intense and the new dance began to differ from the original.

Jason says: 'The difference from the Argentine Tango is that this has to be short, sharp and staccato, so the feet really have to attack the floor. You move across the floor in Tango, but you contract the weight into the floor before you move. Also the hold is a little bit more compact than the other ballroom dances. But short, sharp and staccato is really important.'

Quickstep

Embraced and popularised by the African and Caribbean communities in New York, the Quickstep evolved from the classic Foxtrot in the dance halls of the 1920s, when orchestras speeded up the music to make the routines more challenging. It was standardised in 1927 and is now very different from the Foxtrot, featuring Charleston elements such as hops, skips and kicks as the dancers travel across the floor at lightning speed.

Jason says: 'Rhythm, rhythm, rhythm! For me, it's very easy to get wrapped up in doing lots of hops, skips and running around the floor. But the more intricate you can make the timings and the rhythms, the better your Quickstep will be. Always keep your weight over the front part of your foot, so it is as light and fluffy as possible.'

Dance Class: Speciality

From the sensuous ganchos of the Argentine tango to the complex armography of a spicy Salsa, the Speciality dances are sure-fire crowd-pleasers.

Salsa

The Salsa evolved from a style of dance that dates back to the early 1900s and draws heavily from the Afro-Cuban dance styles such as the Mambo and Guaguancó. It became popular with Cubans and Puerto Ricans living in New York in the 1960s, meaning the New York Salsa is considered the original version, but there are many different styles, including the Cuban Salsa and even the London Salsa. Salsa means 'sauce', so plenty of spice is needed.

Jason says: 'Compared to the other dances, the Salsa, as with the Charleston and the Argentine Tango, has no rules. There's a strict technique that the judges adhere to with the other traditional ballroom and Latin dances, but with Salsa it's freer. You can do the accent on the two or you can do the accent on the one. But getting the light, rhythmic action in the Salsa is really important.

'There are a lot of lifts and they have to be effortless. In the shadow position – the side by side – the intricacies of the footwork have to be exactly the same, because you're also trying to get that synchronisation between two people. The partner work, when they're together, has to look really fluid, and you want lots of great armography. Those arms have to be like spaghetti.'

Couple's Choice

Introduced into the *Strictly* syllabus in series 16, the Couple's Choice allows couples to choose a more freestyle dance in the Contemporary, Jazz or Street/Commercial genres.

Jason says: 'Couple's Choice has been an interesting one because there are so many dance styles that can be introduced. The couples have to strongly interpret what they've decided to do so that it becomes crystal clear what we're meant to be watching.

'Storytelling becomes really important during Couple's Choice. You can't be an expert on every single type of dance, so those judges are really going to be interpreting how you're putting across your narrative. Rose and Giovanni's Couple's Choice last year was the epitome of good storytelling, which is what made it so perfect.'

Charleston

Named after the port city of Charleston, South Carolina, the Charleston is based on the Juba, which comprised of rhythmic stomping, kicking and slapping. In the Roaring Twenties, a song of the same name from the Broadway show *Runnin' Wild* helped to make the Charleston into a dance craze for the young, wealthy rebels who railed against the stuffiness of their parents with shorter haircuts, higher hemlines and the wild flailing and flapping of the new dance – hence the name Flappers. Dancer Josephine Baker helped add the zany elements when she danced the Charleston in the Twenties, adding comedy moves like crossing her eyes.

Jason says: 'A traditionalist will say that there doesn't necessarily have to be swivel in the Charleston because the dance is strongly related to the Lindy Hop and all the other dances in that era, so to have light, very fluid action is really important. Fashion really dictated what the Charleston looked like back in the 1920s because skirts were tight to the knees so there was sort of that flick out from the bottom of the legs. Obviously, a swivel action makes it look even better. I think the zany, carefree character is what really brings a Charleston to life. If you have that, you're already halfway there.'

Argentine Tango

The Argentine Tango is seething with passion and drama, and tells an intense story on the dance floor. Like the ballroom Tango, the Argentine Tango originated in the clubs of Buenos Aires among the city's poorer classes and required a more intimate hold than any previous dance had done. It became fashionable in Europe between 1910 and 1920 and was brought into mainstream entertainment by Italian American actor Rudolph Valentino, who performed the dance wearing gaucho chaps in the 1921 movie *The Four Horsemen of the Apocalypse*. It wasn't a hit with everyone – Vittorio Emanuele III, king of Italy from 1900 to 1946, banned the dance from balls at his palace, and German monarch Kaiser Wilhelm II banned his officers from performing the dance while in uniform.

Jason says: 'The Argentine Tango is almost the exact opposite of the traditional ballroom Tango that we see on *Strictly*. If you think of it like a pyramid, the traditional Tango has the width to the top, with the back arched away from each other. When we do the Argentine Tango, the heads are together, so it gives that feeling of intimacy. The top stays very still and then you must have the fluidity in the legs. Because when you're doing all the ganchos (hooking your leg through your partner's) and the flicking actions, they have to be really loose to be able to respond to each other's leads.'

Hamza
Yassin

As a wildlife cameraman and presenter, Hamza Yassin spends much of his time hiding in the undergrowth in remote parts of the country, dressed in camouflage. But he's more than ready to swap his fatigues and hiking boots for a bit of *Strictly* sparkle.

'I'm excited about the costumes,' he says. 'I never get the chance to wear amazing outfits like these. I'm always in camouflage – black, brown and muted colours – so to be *Strictly*-fied is a treat. Bring it on. I'm hoping for hot pink or baby pink – my favourite colours. They'll have to go easy on the glitter, though. Glitter in my beautiful mane is going to be a nightmare and I'll never get it out. In my job, I need to be hidden, and if I'm shining, the animals will see me from a mile away!'

Born in Sudan, Hamza moved to the UK with his family when he was eight. He earned a degree in zoology at Bangor University and a master's in biological photography from Nottingham University before appearing on CBBC's *Let's Go For a Walk*, as Ranger Hamza. Now living in the Highlands of Scotland, he has fronted the documentary *Scotland: My Life in the Wild* and the four-part series *Scotland: Escape to the Wilderness*. Now Hamza can't wait to go wild on the dance floor.

'I love dancing,' he says. 'It might not be to any rhythm, but I love it. It's like how everyone sounds amazing when they sing in the shower because of the acoustics, and I'm exactly the same when I dance at home. I think I can dance but then you see the professionals and I look nothing like those guys, so I'm looking forward to being trained by the best people ever.'

As well as bringing him closer to nature, Hamza's beloved Highlands have taught him a move or two – which might make it onto the *Strictly* floor.

'I do a lot of Highland dancing, a lot of ceilidhs,' he says. 'So I can do Strip the Willow, the Gay Gordons and so on, and I've got my kilt with me so I'm hoping to put a bit of that into the Couple's Choice.'

Former rugby player Hamza, who is partnered with Jowita Przystał, has been preparing for the show by upping his exercise regime, walking daily and doing squats and sit-ups.

'I'm trying to get the fitness back up again because, as a wildlife cameraman, we can happily sit still for 18 hours and not do anything,' he says. 'But after the first rehearsal with Jowita I had to have an ice bath to soothe my legs because they were on fire. So the body is certainly getting a workout and I know for a fact that I'm going be the fittest I've ever been, even in my rugby days.'

As a passionate conservationist, Hamza is hoping to highlight issues that matter to him through the show.

'I hope that if more people get to know me through this amazing platform, I can speak about my love of the natural world and why we need to look after it,' he says. 'If I can get one or two of the 12 million people watching to understand and climb on the same boat as me, that would be amazing.

'Also, I'm severely dyslexic to the extent that I have to get stuff sent on a voice note to me. So for that 15- or 16-year-old kid to become a television presenter, working in wildlife filmmaking and even doing stuff with Sir David Attenborough, shows it can be done. And now I'm on *Strictly*. It's all about representation and showing people you can make it happen. Some of the world's most successful people are dyslexic, so it's nice to have the opportunity to get that message across.'

Jowita
Przystał

Returning

for her second year on *Strictly*, Polish dancer Jowita Przystał is thrilled to be paired with her first celebrity, wildlife cameraman and presenter Hamza Yassin. And she says she was impressed with his progress in his first few days.

'I was so happy when I found out Hamza was my partner and I couldn't believe it,' she says. 'I'm very excited. It is my first time with a celebrity partner so I want to get it right and I really want him to feel good and learn as much as he can.

'Hamza is a dream to work with; he's really patient, he listens to me and he's fast picking up the steps, even when it is a difficult technique. He is full of surprises.'

While his job filming nature in remote places is a long way from the glitz and glamour of the ballroom, Jowita says there are some transferable skills she can make the most of.

'Hamza is fearless, which is a help, and he's also very strong,' she says. 'The camera kit he carries around for his job is the heaviest thing I've actually picked up in my life, so his strength is also a really good asset for us. He can throw me around in those lifts, no problem. We're working on getting his posture right too. In training for our first dance, the Foxtrot, I was using some extra methods like the mop stuck with duct tape to his back, tennis balls under the arms, all of that. He's working so hard to impress.'

As Hamza is a keen Scottish ceilidh dancer who originally hails from Sudan, Jowita plans to incorporate all aspects of his heritage in the routines.

'I haven't seen him do his Highland dancing yet but I would love to incorporate that into the choreography,' she says. 'He has so many things to offer from his Scottish culture and his African culture. He has told me about his family, his roots, which he would love to share with everybody. There are so many amazing things about him that I can use in our dances for the future.'

But it's not all work and no play for the pair, and Jowita is determined Hamza enjoys his *Strictly* journey.

'We have so much fun together and we giggle all the time. He's really funny and we have a similar sense of humour. We also understand each other, so I can tell when he's tired and needs a five-minute break. We're training nine hours a day but the time flies because we're having such a good time.'

Born in Poland, Jowita started dancing at six, trying out cheerleading, ballet and jazz before moving into ballroom and Latin at 12. She went on to become Polish Open Latin Champion.

In 2020, Jowita and partner Michael Danilczuk appeared on *Strictly* after winning *The Greatest Dancer*, and the following year she joined the pro team.

'It was amazing for me to be around such brilliant people,' she says. 'I learned so much from watching the others do their thing. I was so happy to be asked and when it all started, I felt like the luckiest girl in the world just to be around all of those great choreographers. It was a dream.

'This year, I have the same feeling coming back. It still gives me goosebumps.'

As well as dancing on the main show, Jowita danced an American Smooth with Adrian Chiles on the Christmas Special.

'Adrian is the loveliest man in the world, and I will always remember us sitting in Wales in a little hall and having tea together. He told me he couldn't dance and he would be terrible, but our goal was to do the best we could, go there and actually enjoy it. It was Christmas, so it was really festive; his family came to watch it and he danced really well. I was so proud of him, and he was so proud of himself that he did it.'

For many of the dancers, celebrities and judges, the *Strictly Come Dancing* season doesn't end when the Final is won. Long before the glitterball is handed over to the new champion, plans are laid to take *Strictly* to the people – in the Live Tour that kicks off in January.

The 2022 tour saw seven couples performing their iconic routines in 33 shows, staged at nine venues across the UK. Finalists Rose Ayling-Ellis and Giovanni Pernice and John Whaite and Johannes Radebe were joined by Sara Davies and Aljaž Škorjanec, Rhys Stephenson and Nancy Xu, and Tilly Ramsay and Nikita Kuzmin, from series 19, plus previous contestants Max George, dancing with Katya Jones, and Maisie Smith, who partnered Kai Widdrington.

For John Whaite, the tour was a riot – and a way to wean himself off the magic of *Strictly*.

'The tour was brilliant,' he says. 'It's like all the best bits of *Strictly* rolled into one. You've got the dancers, you've got a huge audience, you've got the friendship backstage and yet there's none of the pressure of having to learn a new dance every week.

'It's also a lovely way to conclude my *Strictly* stint because, when the series finished, I knew I'd miss it, so the tour is like one long four-week goodbye.'

It Takes Two presenter Janette Manrara hosted the show, and Bruno Tonioli made a triumphant return on the judges' panel, alongside Shirley Ballas and the Live Tour's Director Craig Revel Horwood.

Such a huge production requires months of planning and Craig begins devising the show even before the first dance of the series, thinking up ideas for the set and putting the wheels in motion as early as July.

'We start with meetings about content, initially monthly, then every two weeks,' he reveals. 'I come up with a design for the stage, deciding what I want in terms of ramps, steps, raised elements, etc. This year, for example, I chose to make the dance floor black, rather than the traditional wood, then I made the centre stage and satellites black with lighting rings around them, to make it look more studio-like.'

The changes to the set are overseen by Production Director Andy Gibbs, who comes on board in September to put Craig's ideas into action.

'This year the inspiration for the candelabras was from Buckingham Palace,' says Craig. 'I got pictures of them and sent them to Andy, saying, "It needs to be royal, regal, fabulous!" It's his job, then, to go and get it made.

'For the last three years we've had massive Austrian drapes, so this year we decided to have something different and we brought a big white kabuki curtain in,' says Andy. 'The dancers could do shadow work behind it at the opening to the show – it was very dramatic.'

As the main series gets underway, the Tour organisers begin to eye up the talent for the show and take note of the dances that will work well.

By November, the cast are in place and the dances they will perform are being chosen.

'The couples can suggest their favourites but we also try and get a mix, because we don't want seven Argentine Tangos,' Craig says. 'We had to have Rose and Giovanni's Couple's Choice as the final dance, because it was so powerful, but we loved their Argentine Tango so we put that in Act One. Rhys's Charleston was a must because that was just spectacular, and John and Johannes's pirate Paso.

'There were a lot of incredible dances, which meant there were a lot of 10s – even from me!'

Tour Manager Robert Hayden, who brings dancers and celebrities together in early January to begin rehearsals, says the celebrities' favourite styles are also taken into account.

'The show is structured around the best dances to show them off,' he says. 'On tour, we're here to entertain and to showcase their talents.'

Moving from city to city, and constructing the set in different arenas every few days, requires a slick operation, and Andy, who has worked on the tour for 15 years, has the timings down to a tee.

'The set has to go in fast, so everything is designed to be fitted quickly and efficiently,' he says. 'So at The O2 in London, for example, we start at 7 a.m. and everything's done by 2 p.m.

'We've got 16 trucks of equipment and 134 cast and crew travelling with the show. The crew travel in four buses, which we live and sleep on occasionally.'

When the run is finished, the team can dismantle the set and load it onto the trucks in three hours. Andy has a team of 60 crew, and at each venue they're joined by 60–70 local crew from the area, and if the first show at an arena is a matinee, every minute counts.

This year, inspired by *Strictly* champion Rose, the screens at the side of the stage, which beam close-ups to the audience, also had a British Sign Language interpreter to translate the conversations to deaf fans at the arena.

Rose hailed the decision as a huge step for inclusion and says many of her friends felt able to come to the show.

'There were interpreters before for certain shows, but the fact that deaf people can come at any time to any show and it's accessible is really great,' she says. 'The interpreter's screen is huge so they can sit in any seat, which means you don't have to be right at the front.

'It's incredible. A lot of my friends came – 25 of them – and they're all deaf. That is the whole point of *Strictly* for me.'

Although the judges vote, their scores are merely guidelines on the tour and the audience, voting from their seats, choose the winners. While the dances remain the same throughout the tour, there are differences in each performance, giving the judges something fresh to comment on each night.

As well as the couple dances, the audience were entertained with incredible group numbers, choreographed by Creative Director Jason Gilkison, which also featured pros Neil Jones, Luba Mushtuk, Amy Dowden, Nadiya Bychkova, Cameron Lombard, Jowita Przystał and Jake Leigh.

Craig – who has been directing the Live Tour for 11 years – says he loves to keep *Strictly* fans entertained.

'We are constantly changing ideas and mixing it up,' he says. 'What makes the show is the fantastic company and this year they are amazing. It's been a fantastic experience for everybody.'

Tour Manager Robert has nothing but praise for Craig's vision and the work he puts into the show. 'The live show is a celebration of dance,' he says. 'It's funny and entertaining and highlights the talent of all the people involved. The show is quite something.'

Kaye Adams

Kaye Adams has made a successful career out of chatting to everyone from prime ministers to her fellow *Loose Women* panellists, but now it's time to let her feet do the talking. And the journalist and presenter says no one is more surprised than she is to find herself on the dance floor.

'I never saw myself in *Strictly* because I don't see myself as this glamorous, sequinned person,' she says. 'So, actually, when I was asked, it was a genuine shock! But then I thought, "Am I going to regret it if I turn this down?" It would be easy to turn it down because of my own insecurities, but I'd be kicking myself when the show started in September.

'It really is a leap in the dark for me, but the one word that I would attach to *Strictly* is joy – I think the show is about joy, and who's going to walk away from that?'

Kaye, who hosts the podcast *How To Be 60*, says her age was a factor in her decision to take part.

'I set up the podcast because I turn 60 at the end of the year, which, I'll be honest, freaks me out,' she says. 'I'm trying to figure out how you are supposed to be at this stage in your life. What are you supposed to be? When this came along, it just felt right. Rather than closing things down, I saw it as an amazing opportunity, whatever comes of it. It's going to be an incredible experience.'

Scottish star Kaye studied economics and politics at Edinburgh University before becoming a trainee graduate at Central Television, where she scored an hour-long interview with Prime Minister Margaret Thatcher. She went on to host discussion show *Scottish Women* for six years, from 1993, then became chair of *Loose Women* until 2006, returning to the show in 2013.

Partnered with Kai Widdrington, Kaye says he has already made her feel more at ease as she faces the challenges ahead.

'Kai is an absolute revelation,' she says. 'He's 27 years of age but he's so mature, so professional and so talented at what he does, and he's got such a great sense of humour. Even in the first 24 hours he settled me, so I'm really grateful for that and I'm really happy he's my dance partner.'

Kaye's previous dance experience is limited to Scottish country dancing at school, and she says her one and only dance class ended in disaster.

'I actually got thrown out of ballet class when I was five,' she laughs. 'The dance teacher told my mum that I might be better at doing something else as I have kipper feet … whatever they are.'

Now Kaye says one of her biggest challenges will be learning to let herself go on the dance floor.

'I just need to loosen up a bit,' she says. 'I mean, it's the irony of a *Loose Woman* that I've always been quite a reserved person. I am not that good at letting go and strutting my stuff. It's not my natural instinct!'

While she's embracing everything *Strictly* as she goes into the competition, and says she can't wait to get into the posh frocks, Kaye is not clearing a space on the mantelpiece just yet.

'The only eye I have on the glitterball will be to make sure I don't trip over it and smash it by mistake,' she says. 'I'd keep it out of my way to be on the safe side, just in case!'

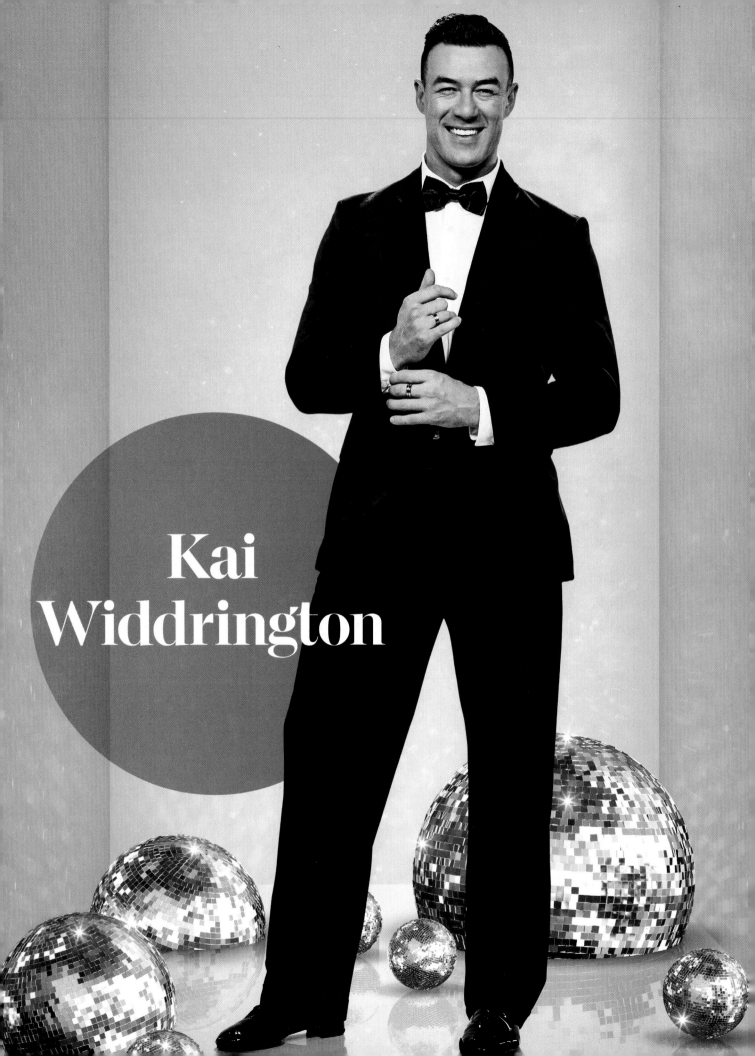

Kai Widdrington

Kai Widdrington made an impressive *Strictly* debut last year with presenter AJ Odudu and he's raring to go with his new partner, journalist and broadcaster Kaye Adams. Their pairing was revealed at the Kelvingrove Art Gallery and Museum, in Kaye's native Glasgow, and they got straight to work with training.

'Kaye has taken to it like a duck to water,' he says. 'She's a natural. I was delighted when I found out it was Kaye. We're getting on like a house on fire, chatting all the time, and she is really putting the hard work in. She's giving it a right good go and I think she's surprised herself by how much she can achieve in such a short amount of time. She's doing an incredible job in my opinion. She really wants to do well, which is all I can ask, so I'm delighted.'

As a journalist, rather than an actor or musician, Kaye has no experience of dancing or playing a role, but Kai says he has his own tricks to help her embody the character of the dance, starting with their week-one Tango.

'The Tango is very dramatic so the way to approach it is to create a character for Kaye,' he says. 'She's not in her comfort zone, but we're trying to get her to be comfortable being uncomfortable. She's very confident when she's interviewing people and hosting shows, and if she can take a bit of that confidence and transfer it to dancing, that would be ideal, so we're working on that.'

Southampton-born Kai began dancing at 12 and two years later became the 2010 World Junior Latin American Champion. At 16, Kai reached the final of *Britain's Got Talent*. He went on to partner celebrities in Ireland's *Dancing with the Stars*, where he was a two-time finalist, before joining the UK show last year. He and AJ made it all the way to the Final but sadly had to withdraw before they could compete, due to injury.

'We had the whole roller-coaster *Strictly* experience – top of the leaderboard one week, in the dance-off the next, then making the Final and having to withdraw,' he says. 'It was very emotional for AJ because she had worked so hard to get there and all she ever wanted to do is dance in the *Strictly* Final. I tried to be strong for her, but I ended up being the one that was crying on national television!

'AJ was great as a pupil, full of enthusiasm and positive energy, and that showed on the dance floor. I really pushed the boundaries with choreography and she wasn't afraid to give it a go. She had genuinely never danced before in her life and what she achieved was incredible. It goes to show what you can do when you put hard work in and trust your teacher. I'm so proud of what we did.'

Kai loved the couple's Charleston, Argentine Tango and Jive, among many other brilliant routines, but he says their Semi-final Quickstep was the most memorable moment for him.

'The Quickstep was like the icing on the cake because the week before, the Quarter-finals, we were in the dance-off,' he says. 'Then AJ pulled out this Quickstep I'd never seen her dance before and she managed to look like she'd been dancing for 10 years. We got our first perfect 40 and it all fell into place.'

Having been through his first dramatic *Strictly* journey, Kai is going into his second year armed with more knowledge of what to expect.

'It's my second series and I feel a little bit more relaxed this year,' he says. 'Kaye is putting in the hard work and dedication and she wants to learn to dance and have fun along the way. So I'm looking forward to the whole series – and I want to actually dance in the Final this time!'

You've Got the Love

With their pirate Paso and their romantic Rumba, John Whaite and Johannes Radebe went down a storm with *Strictly* fans. But as the show's first all-male couple, they did more than just entertain a nation. Their ground-breaking partnership saw their dances voted through every week and joining eventual winners Rose and Giovanni in the most diverse Final to date.

'Being embraced by the public was one of the most reassuring and surprising things for both me and Johannes,' says John. 'The outpouring of love was overwhelming. It made me feel like society really has moved on. For two men to be dancing on primetime television, and for it to be pretty much unquestioned, is remarkable. I feel so humbled to have been part of that.'

The pairing followed hard on the heels of the first all-female pairing, Nicola Adams and Katya Jones, who bowed out in week four the previous year. The former *Bake Off* winner had no dance experience and initially doubted that he and Johannes had the ingredients for a perfect match.

'The physical challenges are different when it's two men dancing together,' he says. 'It was a big challenge for Johannes, because he's used to dancing with a much smaller, daintier person.

I'm six foot two and was 16 stone at the time of filming, so it was difficult for him to choreograph dances that suited my body and would make me look elegant. But he is a great teacher, and we did some beautiful routines.'

The pair started with a bang, grabbing an impressive 30 for their week-one Tango, but John says the week-two Cha-cha-cha was when he found his feet.

'I realised I can pick up choreography and I can dance if I put my heart and soul into it and don't hold back. That was a turning point in the competition and in life, because it gave me a newfound confidence.'

As his confidence grew, so did the judges' scores, with the week-three Paso Doble landing the first 39 of the series.

'The Rumba was my favourite dance because it was so romantic and passionate, and I also loved the Argentine Tango. People thought they were beautiful. They saw two people, regardless of gender or sexuality, working their behinds off to create a beautiful piece of art. That's what we came to do.'

John said he was completely calm on the night of the Final.

'As we started our showdance, I saw Johannes crying, because it meant so much to him in terms of acceptance and representation. I still get emotional talking about it.

'It hit me on the way home. I cried my eyes out for 220 miles back up the M6. I felt like the world is changing and it was very humbling to be part of that. So many people from the community have said, "Thank you," including the older generation who fought for their rights and paved the way for us to do that. It's beautiful to be able to honour those men and women.'

Since the Final, the couple have danced in the *Strictly* Live Tour and John says he has made friends for life with his fellow dancers on the show.

'This time last year, I didn't know where my life was going and then I found myself dancing in the biggest arenas across the UK,' he says. 'If ever there was a moment during the tour where I was feeling a bit tired, I would look in the mirror and say, "Snap out of it, this is never going to happen again." The dancers get to do it year on year, but we have one shot at this little moment of sparkling fabulousness!

'*Strictly* has been a once-in-a-lifetime opportunity. It was hard work, but it was incredibly good fun and I absolutely loved it.'

Motsi Mabuse

Bringing her expertise to the *Strictly Come Dancing* judging panel for the fourth time, Motsi Mabuse can't wait to see what the class of '22 will bring to the floor. But first she has some advice on what makes a *Strictly* champion.

'The first thing is being able to connect with your partner, which is crucial,' she says. 'Then you have to connect to the dancing, fall in love with the dancing, bring in some special charisma of your own and open yourself up completely to the show. If you do, people will see that you're giving your best. If you're authentic and you work hard and give absolutely everything to break through those barriers, I think that's how you win over the judges and the audience.'

The South African-born judge, who also competed in Germany and won the national Latin championship, has been casting an eye over the new intake and she likes what she sees.

'The line-up this year is wonderful,' she says. 'They are very different people from all walks of life, but there are a lot of strong personalities there. They all look like they have potential and it feels like we are in for a brilliant series.'

Having danced at Blackpool during her competition years, Motsi is looking forward to returning to the Tower Ballroom and says it has a special resonance for the dancers.

'For every single one of us in our dance industry, Blackpool is an iconic venue and event,' she says. 'The first time I went in Blackpool, with *Strictly*, I remember the atmosphere was completely different, with the incredible ballroom and bigger audience. I'm very excited about that week. I also love Musicals Week, because I'm a huge fan of musicals, and I love Halloween Week because we get to dress up in fabulous scary costumes.'

Motsi says the BBC has always been a part of her life and she welcomes the centenary celebration.

'The BBC is an international brand,' she explains. 'It is monumental that there's been 100 years of the BBC and it is a part of everybody's daily life. This is a great way to honour that.'

This year also sees a record number of pro dancers taking to the floor, with four new additions in Vito Coppola, Carlos Gu, Lauren Oakley and Michelle Tsiakkas.

'I'm always looking forward to new talents because they change the vibe,' says Motsi. 'They bring a freshness and ambition and they mix things up, so it's exciting to see them dance.'

Motsi is keen to get to know the new cast too and offer words of encouragement and advice.

'I'm looking forward to seeing how it all feels when everybody's back in the studio together and when we get back to Blackpool, with the audience back,' she says. 'I just love it when we start seeing what the cast can do and you start connecting with the personalities. That's when it really starts being fun.'

Motsi says a slice of *Strictly* on a Saturday night is something that brings the family together.

'*Strictly* is all about being there for people, and having a room at home where everybody meets and watches the dancing and bonds as a family. It's about enjoying time together and doing something special.'

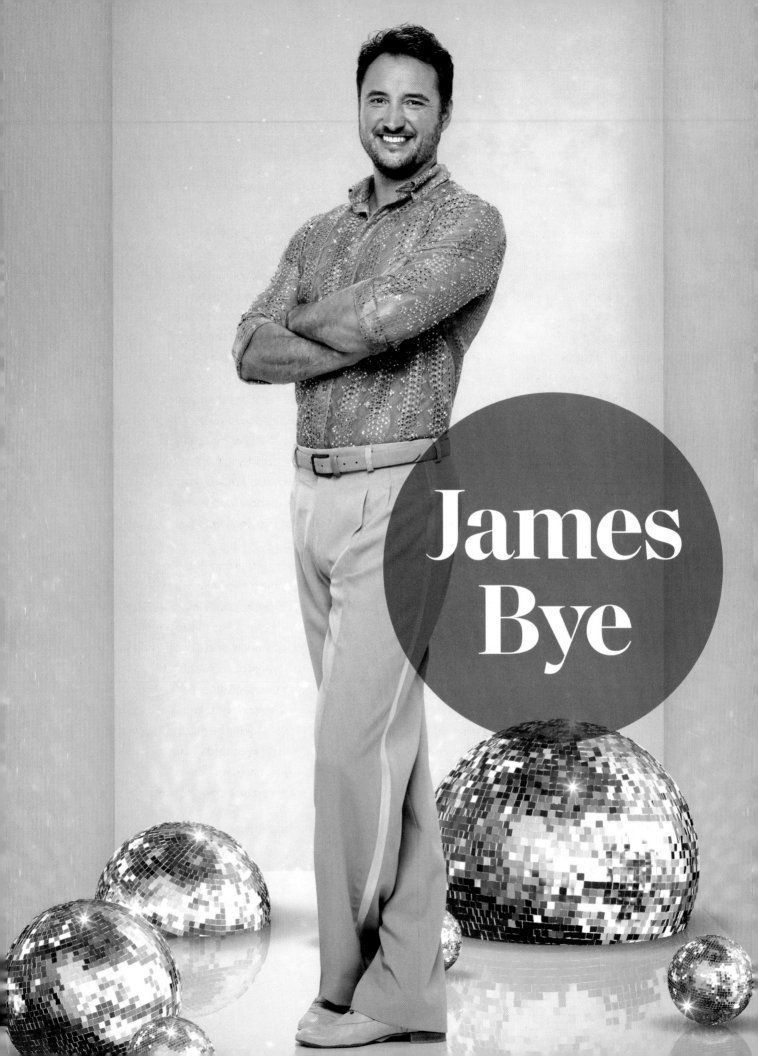

James
Bye

As *EastEnders* barrow boy Martin Fowler, James Bye spends his day flogging fruit and veg to the residents of Albert Square. Now that he's swapping the apples and pears for the famous *Strictly* stairs, he's looking forward to getting glammed up with fake tan and sequins.

'I do that on a Saturday night anyway, so it's nothing different for me,' he jokes. 'But seriously, taking *Strictly* on is not just about the dance, it's the whole thing – the outfits, the fake tans, the Cuban heels. So bring it on. I'm going to enjoy this as much as I can and embrace it all.'

The Basingstoke-born actor starred in *The Great Train Robbery* and *The Hooligan Factory* before taking over the role of Martin in the BBC soap in 2014. In signing up for *Strictly*, he follows in the impressive footsteps of fellow *EastEnders*, including finalists Maisie Smith, Kellie Bright and Emma Barton and current champion Rose Ayling-Ellis.

'They've all been ringing me up and giving me advice about the show,' he says. 'The general consensus is just to have fun and embrace every moment because you just don't know how long it's going to last.

'Obviously, people like Rose, Maisie and Emma were lucky enough to get to the Final, but I'm not them. There's a little bit of pressure and I want to do them proud. Rose said, "Just go and enjoy it," and I'm not a very competitive person so as long as I beat her I'll be fine!'

James is a dance novice and says he has 'no idea if I could be a good dancer or not'.

'I did take part in *Children in Need* with *EastEnders* four years ago, where we did a little choreographed dance,' he adds. 'But I ended up in A&E as my meniscus snapped and I was rushed off for knee surgery.

'People say the acting will help. My worry is that I will either do one or the other – so I'll have the acting nailed or the dancing, and I don't know when the two will come together.'

Making sure it all comes together on the night will be James's dance partner, Amy Dowden.

'Amy comes across all "so nice to meet you" and she's so gentle and sweet, but when you're her dance partner, there is another side where she's like, "Let's get down to business,"' he jokes. 'But I'm so happy that she's my partner because she's brilliant and so supportive. We get on really well.'

While his family, who are Arsenal fans, are excited he is in the show with former player Tony Adams, James is enjoying bonding with all his fellow competitors.

'I think everyone is amazing and the team have done an incredible job this year. We've got a completely varied group, but we are all getting on really well and everyone's really supportive of each other. For me, that's an important part of the show, making a whole new group of mates that are all going through this incredible experience together.'

James says one reason for taking part in *Strictly* was to show his three young sons that 'with a bit of hard work and perseverance you can achieve anything. I guess if I can show them that Daddy can do just one dance well then I've done my job.'

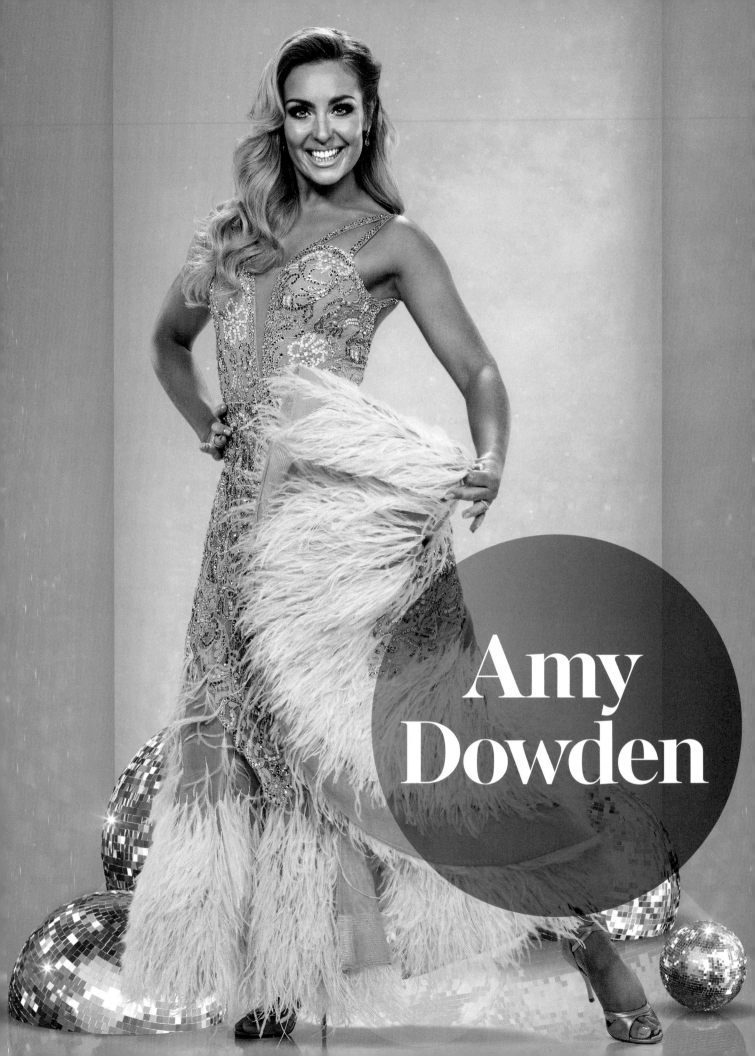

Amy
Dowden

Former finalist Amy Dowden is paired with *EastEnders* star James Bye, and is hoping he will make it as far as his Albert Square neighbour and current champ Rose Ayling-Ellis. So far, she is impressed by his dedication.

'James is still filming and has a gruelling schedule on *EastEnders*, but when he comes into the studio he's so focused and positive – he's an absolute joy,' she says. 'He really wants to learn to dance, he's got a great attitude and the hours we do have are so productive. He's working really hard.'

The couple are kicking off with a Jive and, while James is a dance-floor novice, Amy has spotted plenty of potential for some spectacular moves.

'James has no dance experience, but I've got to say, I do think there's a dancer inside of him. He's really surprised me. In the run-up to *Strictly*, he was going to the gym a lot so he's got good physical stamina, plus he's really strong so I'm looking forward to being able to do dances with lifts.'

As each dance style tells a different story, Amy is also planning to put James's acting skills to work.

'Every week, I like to invent a new character and a new story for our dance, and I think that will help show off his talent,' she says. 'At the moment, we're in the training room and concentrating on the steps, but I'd definitely love to bring his acting skills into the dance and I think it will be a massive asset for James.'

As well as making him the best dancer possible, Amy says her priority is making sure her partner has fun.

'When you go to school, you get the most out of the lessons you enjoyed, and I want James to fall in love with dancing,' she says. 'He's smiling, he's loving it and itching to get back into the studio and, for me, the most important thing is we're having fun as well as getting the job done. We're becoming really good friends. I've met his lovely wife, Victoria, and three children, and he's such a

family guy. And that's exactly what I'm all about as well, so it's perfect. I want the entire family to enjoy his *Strictly* adventure.'

Born and raised in Caerphilly, Wales, Amy has danced since she was eight and is a four-time British National Finalist and a British National Champion. She joined *Strictly* in 2017 and reached the Final with CBBC presenter Karim Zeroual two years later. Last year she reached week nine with McFly singer Tom Fletcher.

'Tom was a golden pupil – very respectful and hard-working,' she says. 'He was a perfectionist, too, which is a good trait. We giggled a lot and had a really good time. That's so important because it is hard work, but you've got to enjoy the process.

'I loved our week-seven Paso Doble, when we got 10s, and it really surprised me how the matador in him came out. But I loved every single week and watching his family embrace the experience. He was teaching his wife, Giovanna, a few steps each week. But most of all, I just love the friendships I've created with him and Giovanna. They're like a brother and sister to me, and that's what I love about *Strictly*, the lifelong friendships it creates.'

Those friendships came into play when Amy married dance partner Ben Jones at a romantic ceremony in her native Wales this summer.

'Tom Fletcher sang, Brian Conley emceed my wedding and JJ Chalmers was there in the outfit he wore for our Viennese Waltz,' she says. 'It was a proper *Strictly* affair and it was brilliant.'

In the upcoming series, Amy is hoping she'll get to Blackpool Week for a very special reason. 'The date we go back to Blackpool, the 19th of November, is exactly six years to the date that I won my British title there with my husband Ben,' she says. 'So it's going to be a very special weekend for us. But I love every week, I can't lie. I just love *Strictly* through and through!'

Booking the Best

Without the fabulous celebs there would be no *Strictly Come Dancing*, and each year excitement builds as a new cast is unveiled to the nation in the weeks before the series begins. For Talent Executive Stefania Aleksander, who has been booking the stars since 2018, the next series is never far from her mind.

'There's always someone I've read about, seen somewhere or who has been mentioned by one of my godchildren, so there's never really a break,'

says Stefania. 'Once a name is on my wish list, I will just keep trying. For example, I asked Bill Bailey three times and he was always too busy. Finally, in 2020, he was available and he called from a supermarket car park to say he was in, so we were over the moon. It's often about timing – and persistence.'

Working closely with Executive Producer Sarah James, Stefania puts together a list of possible contestants and begins making calls early in the year. After chats with the possible candidates, she begins firming up bookings from April onwards, with the final cast signed off by the summer.

With the show garnering loyal viewers from across all generations, Stefania works tirelessly to make sure there is something for everyone.

'The main objective is to create a Saturday-night entertainment show,' she says. 'It's all about representation – trying to find someone that everyone can champion. In my first year, I booked Joe Sugg, who, because of his social media profile, brought a huge following that wasn't necessarily into Strictly before. Older viewers may not have known him, but they got behind him and he made the Final. There are only 15 places so you can't do everything in one series, but we try to mix it up and make sure that each year brings something fresh to the party.'

While striving for a diverse mix of celebrities is crucial, height and dancing ability are not a factor in the choices the talent team makes. 'We didn't know that the cast of 2021 were going to be brilliant until they hit the dance floor. But the point of the show is learning to dance. The pros are so amazing and can take someone like Dan Walker, who might not volunteer himself on a dance floor at a wedding, and turn him into a semi-finalist. Whatever their level of musicality, they can all learn to dance and be brilliant.'

After booking their celebrities, the creative team go about matching them up with the professional dancers.

'Sarah and I meet the contestants and we ask them what kind of teacher they best respond to. All the professionals are patient, which is the most common response, but some say they want fun, light-hearted teaching methods, while others might prefer a regimented teacher. There's no science behind it. We go on gut instinct.

'Some celebrities are really vocal. Tom Fletcher, for example, told me a dozen times that he wanted Amy, but that's not why he was partnered with her. We make our decisions based on what we think is best for the series, but needless to say, Tom was very pleased.'

Last-minute bookings are unusual and even those that look like a rare coup, such as bagging Olympian Adam Peaty after his gold-medal haul at the Tokyo Olympics, come down to serendipity.

'I booked Adam before he went off to compete,' explains Stefania. 'Because of the time difference, I woke up to the news he'd won gold and I couldn't have been happier! Not only had I booked this incredible Olympian, but by the time he came home he had won two golds and a silver, so that was an added bonus.'

The Strictly cast is such a well-kept secret that each celebrity is given a codename once they're booked – and each year there's a different theme.

'I love cheese, so in my first year everyone was a type of cheese and winner Stacey Dooley was Cheddar,' explains Stefania. 'The following year it was superheroes and Kelvin Fletcher was Aquaboy and the next was fruits, so Bill Bailey was Papaya. Last year was a Disney theme and Rose was Belle. For series 20, it's the nation's most loved pet – dogs. Among the cast we have Great Dane, Husky, Chow Chow, Whippet and Golden Retriever.

'I have a lovely team who help me look after the celebrities during the series, Celebrity Producer Jasmine Fox and Assistant Producer Joe Wheatley. Together the three of us make Team Showbiz!'

A superfan before joining the show, Stefania says landing her current role was 'like winning the lottery'. Now she is working towards filling the floor with her own personal wish list.

'My dream is to get Alan Carr because he's a fan of the show and all-round fabulous, Andrew Garfield, if he ever takes an acting break, as well as Lee Mack, Joanna Lumley, the Little Mix girls, Romesh Ranganathan and Rob Beckett. Finally, I'm determined to get Peter Crouch. I would love him to do the robot on the dance floor!'

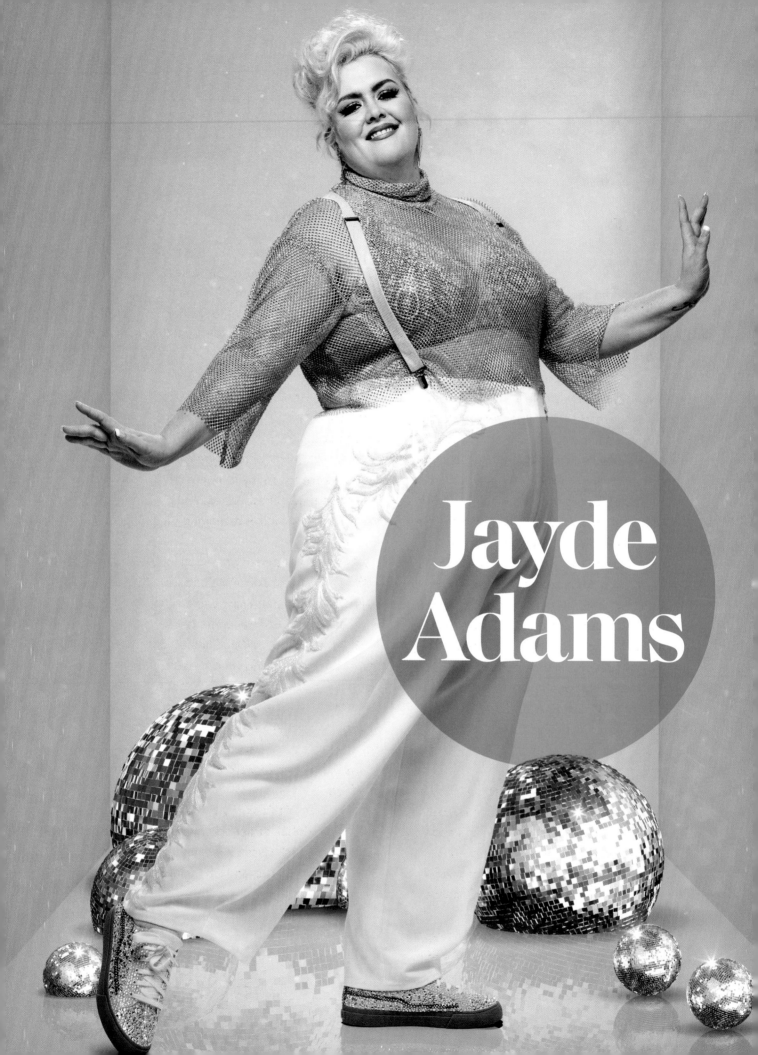

Jayde
Adams

Comedian

Jayde Adams has been a devoted fan of the show since the first series aired in 2004, so walking down the *Strictly* staircase is the fulfilment of a lifelong dream.

'I thought I'd love to be on this show in 2004, after seeing Natasha Kaplinsky win that first trophy,' she says. 'Every single step I've made, every move I've made in my career, was with the idea that I might one day be asked to do *Strictly*. I feel incredibly excited to be doing it. I know how important it is to me, just as a viewer, so I'm not going to waste a single minute of it. Obviously it's going to be hard work, but there's going to be a lot of joy. However long I have on this show, I'm going to make sure every single second counts.'

Bristol-born Jayde began her stand-up career in 2011 and three years later she won the top prize in the Funny Women Awards. Since then she has become a regular on the Edinburgh Fringe, being nominated for Best Newcomer there in 2016, guested on comedy panels including *8 Out of 10 Cats* and hosted Channel 4's *Snackmasters*. The former drama student has also been airing her acting skills more recently, in the comedy *Alma's Not Normal.*

As well as being a *Strictly* superfan, Jayde was keen to take part in the competition to honour her sister Jenna, who tragically died from a brain tumour at the age of 28. The sisters grew up doing synchronised disco dance routines and Jenna had been studying contemporary dance when she was diagnosed.

'It's incredibly emotional and incredibly deep,' she says. 'But there's a sort of beautiful serendipity that I'm on this show. She would have wanted it as much as me. The fact that I get to do this in homage to her is powerful because before she died she said to my mum, "Do you think people will forget me?" Now I get to say her name to millions of viewers on television and I'm really chuffed with that.'

Jayde's favourite dance is the Argentine Tango, and she names Mark Ramprakash's routine with Karen Hardy in 2006 as the best *Strictly* routine ever.

'I'm a massive fan of the Argentine Tango,' she says. 'It is absolutely my favourite bit of the show. There's so much showbusiness and performance in the routine as well as technique – it's really just the best.'

While Jayde has been preparing for the show with 10-mile hikes, swimming and weightlifting, she says the first day of training was a wake-up call. But dance partner Karen Hauer has her back.

'What's great about Karen is she wasn't freaking me out; she was asking what I need to make the partnership better. She's already got training plans and strengthening exercises if she notices a weakness somewhere. She's a fantastic dancer so I'm thrilled to be paired with her.'

Jayde is looking forward to getting into the sparkles.

'I wear a lot of this stuff anyway,' she laughs. 'I did put on a black turtleneck for a little while to get everyone to think I was clever, but it's me going back to the way I was, and I'm thrilled about it.'

Karen
Hauer

As the longest-serving pro, Karen Hauer has a decade of *Strictly* under her belt. As the show celebrates its twentieth series, the Venezuelan-born dancer is welcoming a new challenge, dancing with her first female celebrity in comedian Jayde Adams.

'I was so happy to be paired with Jayde and it was a big surprise because I had no idea that it was going to be an all-woman partnership,' she says. 'It is exhilarating and refreshing. I've had so many different characters, and amazing partners, over the past 10 years, but this feels extra-special. Jayde is an all-round superstar, with astounding energy and charisma, and I love how beautifully confident she is.

'As a partnership, the communication is fantastic. We are both hard taskmasters and we just get the work done, which is great.'

In an all-female pairing, Karen says she's ready to take the lead.

'We get to play with who's the follower and who's the leader at any moment, which is liberating,' she says. 'It's quite beautiful to dance with a woman. It's very sensitive but powerful, and we want to showcase the strength, confidence and the sisterhood in the partnership. We are going to have some amazing routines with a lot of power and storyline behind them.'

'I think Jayde is going to surprise a lot of people and blow them away. As well as her funny side, she's a great actress. So I have so many things I can work with – I'm like a kid in a candy store. They won't know what's hit them when they see Jayde Adams on that dance floor!'

The pair met in Jayde's hometown of Bristol and kicked off rehearsals for their week-one Samba there, and Karen says she's bringing military precision into their training sessions.

'For me, it's about training smart,' she says. 'I believe in pacing yourself and seeing how Jayde reacts on a day-to-day basis. It's about keeping her healthy, looking after her joints and muscles, and that means having the right amount of rehearsal and the right amount of recovery time.'

Jayde is a *Strictly* superfan, with an encyclopaedic knowledge of the show, and Karen sees that as a real bonus.

'If you've watched the show before, it really helps,' she says. 'Jayde knows about the journey that a partnership goes through and what people love to see in the celebrities. It's great that she comes equipped with all this knowledge and it's fun, because she was watching the show before I was on it so she probably knows more than I do! As a pro, it's refreshing to get a celebrity who loves the show as much as we love it.'

Born in Venezuela, Karen began dancing at eight, after moving to New York, and won a scholarship to the Martha Graham School of Contemporary Dance. She studied African, contemporary and ballet before moving on to ballroom and Latin at 19. In 2008 she became World Mambo Champion. She joined *Strictly Come Dancing* in 2012, dancing with Nicky Byrne, and last year partnered actor Greg Wise.

'Greg was lovely. It was great to be able to partner him and, we had some great numbers. He wanted to do the James Bond Paso Doble and also to dedicate a dance to his sister, which was very beautiful and meant a lot to him. We got to meet his wife, Emma Thompson, which was incredible, and I think he thoroughly enjoyed it and had fun. That's all that matters to me.'

Ahead of the new series, Karen is looking forward to dancing in front of the *Strictly* audience once again.

'There is an energy in the room when we have an audience that is quite electrifying,' she says. 'I'm really looking forward to performing in front of an audience in the studio and for Jayde to feel that as well, because dancing on that floor with millions watching at home and people supporting you in the studio is a unique experience.'

Claudia Winkleman

Returning as host on the live shows, Claudia Winkleman is anticipating a cracking series and is enjoying getting to know the new batch of celebrities. And she says reuniting with her *Strictly* colleagues, including close pal Tess Daly, at the launch show was a momentous occasion.

'The launch show was thrilling and we all got quite emotional,' she says. 'It was so exciting to have an audience and it was an amazing show. We've got four new pros who are unbelievable, and this year's cast are brilliant. I love them all.

'Every single one of this new group is tremendous and they're already completely looking after each other.'

After observing them in their first group dance, Claudia says each one has the attitude and drive to become a *Strictly* champion, even though they can't all make it to the Final.

'I was really studying them because normally at that point I'm just trying to eat as many sweets as I can!' she jokes. 'They all looked like they had potential.

'I think what makes a *Strictly* champ is a willingness to dive in and embrace it, and this current group are all fully embracing it. There's nobody who wants to give less than 100 per cent. In my view, you don't necessarily have to lift the glitterball to be a *Strictly* champion. I'd say Ed Balls is a *Strictly* champion, as is Debbie McGee and so many more who have impressed and entertained us on the dance floor.'

As well as the first weeks of dancing, and the themed weeks, Claudia says she is looking forward to heading north for the Blackpool special.

'Blackpool Week is the best thing of all,' she says. 'I feel very strongly about Blackpool and I love it, especially in November, which might sound weird, but never have I been anywhere that welcoming. The Tower Ballroom is just spectacular, but it's the whole town that makes it. They wrap their arms around us. I go to the same place for fish and chips and everyone we meet is smiley. They're so kind to us, so we're very grateful and feel very lucky to go there.'

The presenter is also keen to get back to her 'Clauditorium', where she greets the couples for a debrief after their routines.

'To have more than one couple up with me on my little balcony is making me so happy,' she says. 'After they've done their routine live on TV, the couple don't just want to talk to me, they want the other pros and celebrities for support.'

After Anton's first stint as a judge last year, Claudia is thrilled to see him return and says he offers a new perspective to the panel.

'Anton is a delight, absolutely edible!' she says. 'What's brilliant about Anton is that he's done it. He was part of the pro team so recently, he knows how they feel at every stage of the competition and he always sums it up perfectly.'

Part of the *Strictly* family from 2004, when she first presented *It Takes Two*, Claudia has been hosting the main show with Tess from 2014. As we celebrate the twentieth series, Claudia reflects on the qualities that draw record viewers to the show every year.

'I think the magic of *Strictly* is that it's a snow globe of a show,' she says. 'I think that the celebrities' joy in it all comes through the screen.

'It's incredibly compelling and heart-warming to watch people try. And you can't half try to dance; you have to fully throw yourself in. Alongside that, we have the best professional dancers, the best live band, the most extraordinary judges and the best production team, so it all comes together. We never take for granted that people will come and watch, but hopefully, as in previous years, they will.'

Ellie Simmonds

With five Paralympic gold medals to her name, Ellie Simmonds is used to winning and will be bringing her competitive nature to the *Strictly* party. But the record-breaking swimmer admits she may feel like a fish out of water on the dance floor.

'I think some of my sporting skills will definitely help, like the training routine, the mental side and the competitiveness, but I know that from swimming, and this is out of my comfort zone,' she says. 'I'm used to being in water on my own, which, for me, is mental freedom and somewhere I go to escape. Now I'm on dry land and dancing, not just in front of the audience and the judges, who I totally forgot about until we started rehearsing, but also many people at home. I thought about a million people watched *Strictly*, then someone told me it was 12 million, and I was thinking, "Oh my God!"'

Ellie, who was born with the genetic condition achondroplasia, started swimming at five and, at 13, became the youngest British athlete at the 2008 Paralympics in Beijing, bagging gold in the 100-metre and 400-metre Freestyle. She also became the youngest person to receive an OBE, at 14. She went on to win two more golds at the 2012 London Paralympics and another at the 2016 Rio games. She also has 14 golds from the World Para Swimming Championships. Now retired, Ellie is a presenter for BBC Sport and has also made documentaries, including *Ellie Simmonds: A World Without Dwarfism?*

Having filled her time with training since her early years, Ellie's retirement meant she could grab the chance to try on her dancing shoes and she didn't hesitate to sign up.

'Well, it's *Strictly*, isn't it? It's the show of all shows,' she says. 'I've watched it for years and years with my family, so I've always wanted to do it.

When they asked me this year I had to say yes! After retiring last year I've got more time on my hands, so I can enjoy it. You learn a new skill with the dancing, plus the whole shebang with costumes, make-up, hair, the fake tan and the sequins!'

The swimmer, who grew up in the West Midlands, says glamming up for the show is part of the appeal.

'I am so excited,' she says. 'I'm used to so many years of being in the water, not really caring what I looked like, with wet hair, chlorine-smelling skin, a tracksuit and no make-up. Now to actually enter this world, it's a whole new level with the hair, the make-up, everything! Bring it on!'

Paired with Nikita Kuzmin, Ellie says the series will be a learning curve for both of them.

'Nikita has never danced with an individual with dwarfism before and I've never danced before,' she says. 'So we're just going to have to figure out where I'm putting my hands, how we go into hold and all that type of stuff. It's all new, but it's about adapting and seeing what works. Nikita is open to that, he's an amazing teacher, he's up for a challenge, and I am as well. I want to show that if I can do it, anyone can do it. It is nerve-wracking, but we're both up for it and we're getting on with each other. Plus, he's making me laugh and I love a laugh.'

Ellie's previous dance experience is limited to friends' weddings and nights out, but she's keen to throw herself into learning a new skill.

'When we did the first dance we were all aching afterwards and I thought, "Wow, this is really hard,"' she says. 'But it's all part of it and it's definitely a pinch-me moment when you realise you're doing it for real. It's just amazing. I'm doing *Strictly Come Dancing*. I can't believe it!'

Nikita
Kuzmin

After an impressive debut with Tilly Ramsay last year, Nikita returns to the *Strictly* ballroom with swimmer Ellie Simmonds. And he says the five-time Paralympic gold medallist is already finding her feet on dry land.

'Ellie is lovely and we are getting on really well,' he says. 'She has a competitive mindset so when she's switched on to training, she's properly focused, which is really good. A sporting background helps everybody, whether you did sport as a kid or as an adult, because it gives you the right focus and coordination, which is always welcome.

'Obviously Ellie is used to being in water, but her coordination is very good. The tricky thing is coordinating feet and arms, because it's completely different to swimming and is especially tough on the calves. But she is working so hard.'

While training hard, the couple are also having plenty of laughs, and Nikita reveals an unusual quirk which often stops him in his tracks.

'The fun thing with Ellie is that she just suddenly comes up with random questions,' he says. 'So we're doing the Cha-cha-cha and, completely out of nowhere, she says, "What's your grandmother's middle name?" She's really fun.'

As Ellie was born with dwarfism, Nikita is adapting his choreography to take in their height difference, but he says he is relishing the challenge.

'We have tried a few ways of adjusting the hold to see how it's going to go,' he says. 'The ballroom and Latin present different challenges because, even when you are not in close hold, there are a lot of steps where we would have a different stride, but it's really interesting for me, as a professional, to choreograph to different needs and adapt. I can't remember the last time I've been so excited to come to training and to do choreography. This is a completely new challenge for me so I'm like a little kid who's excited all the time to try something new. It's a great opportunity for both of us.'

Born in Ukraine, Nikita started dancing at four when he failed the entrance to karate club because he couldn't do a forward roll. At nine, Nikita moved to Italy and continued to study dance, becoming six-time Latin and Ballroom National Champion. He later moved to Germany where he appeared on the show *Let's Dance* before joining *Strictly* in series 19 and dancing his way to week 10 with Tilly Ramsay.

'Tilly was the perfect partner to have in the first year,' he says. 'I really couldn't have wished for a better partner and I had a wonderful time. My favourite dance was the Halloween Cha-cha-cha to the song "Spooky Movies", when we were both in green make-up, because that was such a fun week.'

The pair went on to dance in the *Strictly Come Dancing Live!* tour, and Nikita admits he cried through the final show because he didn't want it to end.

'The arena tour was amazing,' he says. 'I remember the first time I came onto the floor, and the kabuki drape fell down from the ceiling to reveal the cast. For the first time, I saw so many people roaring. I'd never seen an audience like it, and that is a moment I'll never forget. It was just beautiful.'

Going into his second series, Nikita says he is still taking new experiences in and is looking forward to going to Blackpool, where he competed many times as a boy.

'I enjoyed every minute of last year and I remember going into it knowing I had a lot to learn,' he says. 'I'm taking it the same way this year, because you always have a lot to learn, realistically, and I'm still learning every single day.

'For my first series, I started with the mindset that you do your best and it's okay if you make mistakes because you're going to learn from them, so don't put pressure on yourself. I had a lot of support from Tilly, from the whole *Strictly* team and my family, so I'm blessed.'

Strictly Quiz

Are you a *Strictly* superfan?
Time to rest your dancing feet and test your
Strictly knowledge with our fun quiz.

Answers on p128

1 Which song did series-18 winner
Bill Bailey perform his showdance to?

2 Anton Du Beke has now taken a seat on the judges'
panel, but who was his first celebrity partner on the show?

Which *Strictly* dance shares its name
with a city in South Carolina? **3**

4 Which soap has now seen three of its stars take the glitterball?

5 Series 19 had the joint-earliest ever perfect score, awarded in week six, but which couple earned it?

6 Which singer won the Christmas special in 2021, with Graziano Di Prima?

7 Which aquatic creature did Dan Walker dress as in Halloween Week?

8 Which country do Cameron Lombard and Johannes Radebe both hail from?

9 Which evil Disney character did Judy Murray dress as for her memorable American Smooth in 2014?

10 Who danced the first routine in 2021?

11 Can you name the two celebrities who shared the series-14 Final with Ore Oduba?

12 Who was the first celebrity to get a perfect score on *Strictly*?

13 Which of the current pro dancers has been on the show the longest, joining in series ten?

14 Which iconic venue does *Strictly* move to for one week in most series?

15 Which motoring presenter wore an L-plate on the dance floor in series two?

Matt
Goss

Bros legend Matt Goss is used to the bright lights of Las Vegas, where he had a resident show for 10 years, and has spent over 30 years in the music industry. But he says the *Strictly* dance floor is a whole new experience and that letting go of the reins in order to learn new skills might be tough.

'I'm always the boss,' he explains. 'In my show there are 50-plus people working together, and I oversee everything from the lighting to the dancers. But for *Strictly* I will be the pupil and, for me, it's quite nerve-wracking. But it's nice to get out of my old ways, because I've been doing what I do for a long time and to come into an environment that is so alien is super-exciting. I'm looking forward to learning a skill from an incredibly talented partner who knows exactly what they're doing.'

While he is used to calling the shots, Matt says he will be putty in the hands of his dance partner, Nadiya Bychkova.

'The pros are so patient and so giving, and at the end of the day you've got to surrender to their knowledge,' he says. 'That's the most important thing you can do.

'Nadiya is fantastic and we're very similar – we get on really well. She is super-patient and kind, and I was very happy when I found out who my partner was.'

Along with twin brother Luke and pal Craig Logan, Matt formed Bros in 1986 and the band went on to become a pop sensation, earning millions of fans with the release of 'When Will I Be Famous?' and following up with a string of hits and the quadruple platinum album *Push*. Matt, who went solo in 1995, has also had five studio albums and, from 2009, a sell-out show at Caesars Palace, Las Vegas, which he also brought to the Royal Albert Hall and Wembley Arena. His stint was so successful he was named the 'new king of Vegas' and the city declared 8 August as official Matt Goss Day. He and Luke also starred in the film *Bros: After the Screaming Stops*, which documented their preparation for their 2017 Bros reunion.

After living in the States for much of the last 25 years, Matt is enjoying his homecoming to the UK and says his fellow *Strictly* celebs have already become part of his life.

'On the first day we all trained together, we connected,' he says. 'We really worked hard, but it was a nice feeling because of the instant camaraderie between us. What they tell you about *Strictly* is actually true – that you bond so well with everyone on it.'

Matt jokes that he is not banking on his musical talents helping him on the dance floor.

'I think there's a misconception that a musical background can give us a head start,' he says. 'We do understand how to make music and the accents and the count. So if we're told to do something on the second beat of the bar, we understand what that means. That does help, but we vocalists feed off an audience, rather than have set moves.'

He may have a mantelpiece full of awards already, but the pop icon is going all out for the most sought-after gong of all.

'Why would I do this wonderful show if I wasn't going to try to get to the glitterball?' he says.

Nadiya
Bychkova

Former Slovenian champion Nadiya Bychkova is paired with Matt Goss for her fifth series on the show, and she couldn't be more excited. She was paired with the singer at The O2 Arena, where his legendary band Bros played a reunion gig in 2017.

'It was very special to film our pairing at The O2 because that's where he came back together with his brother, Luke, for the reunion gigs,' she says. 'I didn't know I was getting him, but I'm so happy to get Matt. He is a superstar and I'm excited to get to know him. He's very kind. A real gentleman.'

As Matt is an international star with hit singles, live performances and even a Vegas residency under his belt, his musical talent is something Nadiya can build on.

'Matt knows music inside out and that's a big plus,' she says. 'He's got rhythm, he's picking up steps well and understands the structure of dance and music, which is really helpful. Obviously it's early days, but I'm enjoying teaching him and he's working so hard. He is giving it his all and that's the best I can ask from anyone I teach.'

As part of her research into her new partner, Nadiya watched the award-winning documentary *Bros: After the Screaming Stops*, and she says she knew some of the band's songs.

'It's incredible how big Bros were, and so many people still love them, so Matt being on *Strictly* is wonderful for his fans,' she says. 'He's coming home from America and he says he is trying to say yes to more and do things he's never done before. This is not his comfort zone but he's doing it, which is a big step for him and it's great for the show, for me and for the fans.'

Nadiya is struck by her new partner's stylish wardrobe and says his fashion sense could be reflected in his *Strictly* costumes.

'I think he'll bring a lot of Matt Goss to *Strictly*, even showing up to rehearsals, he always looks great. There is so much style – he loves fashion and he loves to be different as well, which is great. He loves beautiful things and he loves the small details in everything, from clothes to choreography, which is incredible.'

Born in Luhansk, Ukraine, Nadiya has been the Slovenian Ballroom and Latin Champion multiple times as well as two-time World Champion and European Champion in Ballroom and Latin Ten Dance. She joined *Strictly* in 2017, dancing with actor Davood Ghadami. Last year she reached the Quarter-finals with TV presenter Dan Walker.

'It was a great series for me, and Daniel was incredible,' she says. 'We got on so well and had so much fun. He became a dancer and he still loves dancing.

'As Dan gained confidence, he just wanted to learn more and more dances. For us, every week we stayed in the competition was a gift, and I don't think I have ever seen anyone work as hard as he did, with both *Strictly* and his job. That was what helped us stay so long in the competition. I really enjoyed it and I have an amazing friend for life.'

This year, Nadiya jokes that she's looking forward to dancing 'every week, including the Final'.

She adds: 'Honestly, I just hope we can stay as long as we can in the competition because I love to teach. I'm enjoying teaching Matt and he's loving the process of learning. In our first rehearsals Matt asked me what it was about Blackpool that was so special, so I'd love to take him to the Tower Ballroom to show him. I danced my first ever competition in England there, when I was 10 years old, and for every dancer it is a very special place. It's an amazing week for *Strictly* and I'm definitely looking forward to that.'

Walking Wardrobe

No *Strictly Come Dancing* show would be complete without the sequins and stones of the fabulous costumes, and the Live Tour means thousands of fans get to see the glamorous garments in person.

With seven couples performing individual dances, plus six extra professionals and several group numbers, a total of 200 costumes are transported around the country for the 33 shows. Even the cameramen and some of the crew, who are visible to the audience, have suits for the tour.

While the majority of the couples' outfits come from the main series, with tweaks to make them even more eye-catching for the arena setting, there are also new looks for some of the group dances.

Bryony Clayden, the live show's Head of Wardrobe, has worked on the tour for 11 years and collaborates with *Strictly*'s Head of Costume, Vicky Gill, to make sure all the costumes are fit for the gruelling weeks ahead.

'Ahead of the tour, Vicky's team and my team work together on all the fittings and alterations, applying all the stones and so on. Then she hands it over to me and we take it on the road,' Bryony explains. 'I have a team of six and our job is to dress everyone, make any repairs that need doing, and to keep each outfit looking as fresh as it did on day one, all the way through the tour.'

The costumes fill seven rails, measuring six foot each, and with the dancers putting the outfits through their paces, sometimes for two performances a day, each one has to be washed daily. The wardrobe team travels with three washing machines and three tumble dryers, but, because of the delicate nature of many of the fabrics, and the heavy stoning, not everything can be dried in the usual way.

'There's a lot of washing, ironing and steaming,' says Bryony. 'Most things can't be tumble-dried and we have to get them dried within a really short span of time, so we tour with two huge heated wardrobes. We hang everything inside the cabinets, and they blow hot air through. It dries most costumes within half an hour.'

On matinee days, when there are two shows, Bryony and her team arrive at the arena at 9 a.m. and wash everything that was worn the night before, to make sure they are dry before the afternoon show. Between the two performances

they have as little as two hours to rewash the clothes.

The talented costume team also makes daily repairs to the costumes, as well as hand-gluing thousands of crystals, to keep them at their sparkling best.

'Things get split or torn and everyone in the department can sew to a high level, so we just have to keep repairing everything to keep it looking smart and clean,' says Bryony. 'On the latest tour, Nadiya Bychkova had a dress with a 12-metre train for one group number and somehow that got a huge rip right up the centre, so it all had to be brought in and carefully sewn up, which was one of the biggest jobs on tour.

'By the time we get to the final shows at The O2 the dresses have been through a lot, but we need to keep them looking as sparkling as the first day. Vicky always brings her family to one of the final shows in London, so that's an added incentive to make sure everything still looks amazing!'

While they are busy washing, sewing and sticking, almost to curtain-up, the costume team needs to be on the ball during the performance, to help out with quick changes.

'With so many dancers going from group

numbers to individual dances, some changes are as short as 90 seconds,' says Bryony. 'Everything has to be ready and perfect to avoid hold-ups. It's all hands on deck to make it go as seamlessly as possible.'

For Director Craig Revel Horwood, the stunning costumes are an essential part of bringing the glamour of *Strictly* to fans across the UK.

'One of the great things about the tour is that the audience gets to see the full body during the dance,' he says. 'When you see all the rhinestones in real life it's unbelievably zingy and sparkly.'

When it comes to putting on the glitz, the costume department on the Live Tour, as on the series, have it all sewn up.

Fleur East

As a successful singer, Fleur East is used to being in the spotlight and even throwing a few shapes, but she is a complete novice when it comes to ballroom and Latin.

'A lot of people are saying my being a singer will help, but I haven't been trained and I have never been to stage school,' she says. 'This is me going from winging it, freestyling and singing with a mic in my hand, to dancing like a professional, so I'm going to be thrown into the deep end and it's going to be really different for me.'

While she is looking forward to the faster Latin dances, Fleur is a bundle of energy and says she might find it hard to slow down for the slower numbers.

'When I'm performing, a lot of my songs are high tempo and that's where I'm comfortable,' she says. 'So with a Waltz or a really calm ballroom dance, where I have to be controlled and graceful, I don't know how I'll be. I've never had to do anything like that so it's going to be challenging.'

The Londoner, who shot to fame as a finalist in *The X Factor* in 2014 before releasing two albums, currently fronts the breakfast show on Hits Radio. Although she's looking forward to the fun side of her new challenge, Fleur has a poignant reason for taking on the *Strictly* contest.

'Firstly, it's the best show ever, but secondly, for me, it's a personal reason,' she says. 'My dad passed away in 2020 and this was his favourite show. He even used to get annoyed that he had to miss out on *Strictly* when I was on *The X Factor*

because they were on at the same time. When I was deciding whether or not to do it, I spoke to my sister and she reminded me of Dad watching it all the time, so that was the deciding factor straight away. He's my motivation for doing it.'

Partnered with new dancer Vito Coppola, Fleur says she's prepared to work hard in pursuit of the elusive glitterball trophy.

'When I met Vito I said, "Just tell me what I need to do. I'm here to learn,"' she says. 'We're pretty similar in our energy; we laugh a lot, but when it comes to dancing, we're both really focused.

'I think he's going to be firm with me, but I need that because I'm learning a completely different style that I don't know. We're going to work hard but have a lot of fun at the same time.'

To prepare for the show, Fleur has been working out and building up her stamina for the tough training ahead.

'There's no point in me trying to master a Waltz in my living room – I wouldn't even know where to start! So the only thing I can do is work on my physical fitness, because I know that it's going to be hardcore.

'I started looking at *Strictly* videos to get into the vibe of the show and I saw the places celebrities were putting their legs. One dancer had her leg up by her ear, so I thought, "Okay, I need to stretch!"'

As well as learning the dances, the talented star is looking forward to donning the sparkly dresses and says she's been in training for being *Strictly*-fied all her life. 'I can't wait!'

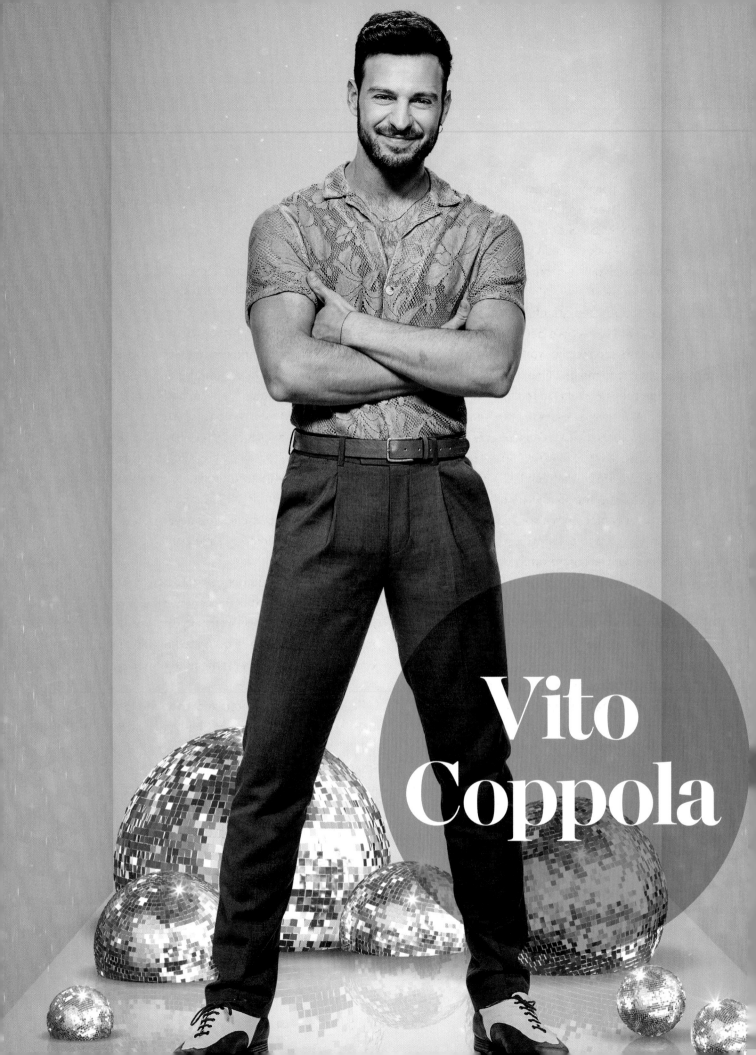

Vito
Coppola

New pro Vito Coppola joins the team as reigning winner of *Ballando con le Stelle*, Italy's version of *Strictly Come Dancing*, and he also has 11 national Latin championship titles under his belt. Now he's thrilled to be making his debut on the UK show.

'I'm very happy and grateful,' he says. 'I know how lucky I am to be here because there are many good dancers around the world and the *Strictly* producers chose me because they saw something in me that they liked, so I'm really grateful for that. Joining *Strictly* is a pleasure and an honour. The launch show for me was electrifying. Everything is new and exciting, and while I knew it would be good, it was even better than I expected.'

Born in Eboli, in the southern Italian region of Salerno, Vito comes from a sporting family, with a gymnast mum and a dad who was an acrobatic rock 'n' roll dancer before opening his own dance school. 'Everybody dances in my family,' he says. 'My brother is the Italian champion of another discipline and my cousins, aunts, uncles all dance. Even my grandparents still go to dance twice a week.'

At six, Vito began lessons – after his mum decided he needed to channel his considerable energy. 'I was quite hyperactive, always dancing around my house and being annoying, and Mum wanted to tire me out. So I went to dance school and never looked back. Because my father was the coach, he was really tough on me, but I think if he hadn't been I would not have been here today.'

A year later, Vito began competing and at the age of nine he won the first of his many Italian championships. At 11, he was called to join the Italian team in the International Championships in Germany and he went on to become World Champion and European Champion, as well as winning the European Cup, World Cup and Grand Slam. In 2020, he left the competitive circuit and was asked to dance in last year's *Ballando con le Stelle* (*Dancing with the Stars*), coming first with singer Arisa.

When he got the call from *Strictly*, Vito's family were over the moon – although his mum was a little emotional about his move to the UK.

'Everybody was really happy for me. My father, who is very career orientated, didn't hesitate to say, "Go," and my brother, who is my biggest supporter, was excited. My mum had tears in her eyes but she told me, "As long as you are happy, go for your dream and enjoy it." I have a huge family and I call them every day. I'm hoping they will come over for the live shows.'

Vito is paired with singer Fleur East and says he is seeing plenty of potential in his new dance partner.

'She is a hard worker and she wants to practise and improve.'

'After the first group dance, I told her to rest for a couple of days. But she sent me a picture because she was doing stretching exercises in preparation. I think we're going to have so much fun because we have the same level of energy and she gives me positive vibes.

'Fleur is very coordinated and, even though she's never done a Samba, Jive or Cha-cha-cha before, I think she might feel more confident in the Latin. She's a hard worker, so I think she's going to smash it.'

While the Italian champ would love to continue his winning streak, he is not counting his chickens.

'I'd love to lift the glitterball on my first year, and everybody wants to win,' he says. 'As it's my first year, my goal is to show what I'm able to do and to help my celebrity improve as much as possible. To arrive at the Semi-final, then the Final, would be a huge goal to achieve. After that, if people support us and vote for us to win, of course I don't mind!'

Janette Manrara

After an eight-year run on the main show, Janette Manrara moved on to pastures new last year, staying in the *Strictly* family on *It Takes Two*. For the American-born professional, who took over from Zoe Ball, it was a dream come true.

'I remember when I first came onto *It Takes Two*, with my first celebrity, Julien Macdonald, I thought, "This is the dream job,"' she says. 'It was the epitome of what I wanted to do next. When I met the whole team and Zoe, we had the loveliest chat and I felt looked after by everyone. It was definitely a pinch-myself moment when I walked into that studio as the new presenter.'

This year, Janette is looking forward to welcoming all the couples to the *It Takes Two* studio again.

'I'm super-excited for the cast because there are some really great names,' she says. 'I'm looking forward to getting to meet them and know them better. It looks like it's going to be a great series.'

During her time on *Strictly*, Janette partnered Aston Merrygold, Will Bayley and Jake Wood. She went out with a bang in series 18, getting to the Final with singer HRVY and breaking the record for the earliest perfect score, with their week-six Street/Commercial routine. While she had a blast throughout her time on the show, she says the timing of the move was perfect.

'I'm 39 this year and I'm not going to stop dancing, ever, but you have to look forward to what's next in your career at some point,' she says. 'It's nice to know that I can do something that makes me just as happy as dancing.'

As she and Rylan split the show throughout the week, their paths rarely cross, but that hasn't stopped her co-host being a huge support.

'Rylan is such an amazing co-host and we've become really great friends and we text each other all the time,' she says. 'He was so kind, warm and lovely, and gave me so much support.'

Janette says after the move she still felt firmly in the *Strictly* camp. 'I'm lucky that I'm such good friends with the pros, and I was talking to them most days,' she says, 'and being on *It Takes Two* meant I met the celebrities, which made me happy. I helped with choreography for a couple of group numbers too, so I got to work with the pros in a different capacity. It was a nice transition.'

Now she has stepped away, Janette is able to share her own tips and experiences to help the competing couples. 'I'm living vicariously through them. Listening to what they're going through and their stories reminds me of similar things happening to me, so it's nice to support them and give them a sounding board. I hope that when they sit down opposite me, they feel really relaxed and comfortable and can just have a good chat.'

She also loves to encourage and nurture the newer additions to the pro team on the show.

'They seem like such a nice bunch and they're incredibly talented so I'm excited to see them in action. With all the pros I say, "I'm there for you if you need me. My door is always open."'

As well as presenting *It Takes Two*, Janette hosted the *Strictly Come Dancing Live!* tour when it went on the road from January, and she loved her role in the show.

'I felt like I just slipped right in, because I've done the tour for many years,' she says. 'Playing to huge audiences in arenas was wonderful. To come out every night and hear that roar from them is an indescribable feeling. *Strictly* fans are the best in the world, because they're so loving, kind and supportive of everyone in the show. They're just the best people to perform to.'

Tony
Adams

Having captained both Arsenal and England, former footballer Tony Adams loves being on the winning team and has a fierce competitive streak. Now he's hoping his stuffed trophy cabinet will soon have a new addition.

'Of course I've got my eye on the glitterball. I've never been in any competition that I've not wanted to win,' he says.

The sportsman and TV personality, whose playing career spanned 22 years, says the timing is just right for this year's *Strictly* after he retired from his role as manager of Granada in 2017.

'Recently I've decided to put my feet up and watch my kids grow up, so I can do anything I want. So I have decided to learn a new skill in dancing. It looks like a fun show so I am looking forward to it.'

Born in Romford, Tony joined Arsenal as a schoolboy, making his first team debut weeks after his seventeenth birthday, and he spent his entire professional career at the club. He captained the team to become the first English side to win the League Cup and FA Cup double in the 1992/1993 season, and went on to lead the England squad to the semi-finals of the '96 Euros, when they lost on penalties to Germany. He has made a record 60 appearances at Wembley and is still the only England player to make tournament appearances in three separate decades. Tony's battle with alcoholism was documented in his bestselling book *Addicted* and led him to set up the charity Sporting Chance, which helps athletes struggling with addiction. His charitable work is part of the reason he wanted to take on the *Strictly* challenge, and he also believes dancing can help boost mental health.

'I've been without a drink or drug for 26 years so the charity is helping others in the position I was in and spreading awareness,' he says. 'On *Strictly*, I want to prove you can do anything when you're free of addiction.

'When I set up my charity, particularly the rehab side, I thought it made sense to do physical exercise as well as the one-on-one therapy and group therapy. They are athletes, and I know that when I go for a run and have a shower I feel like a different person, so I quickly put 12 sport therapies alongside the mental health therapies we offer and one was dance. We've had a dancer coming to the rehab centre for the last 22 years doing dance therapy, because it's great for you. Give it a bash.'

Tony, who is paired with Katya Jones, admits to being slightly nervous about taking to the floor and says his dance experience amounts to 'freestyling a bit at Ilford Palais in about 1981'.

'The first rehearsal was like the first day of school because we were all a little bit scared,' he says. 'I did one little freestyle dance and Katya joked, "Whatever that was, I don't want to ever see it again!"'

The England legend and dad of five says his family will be cheering him on from the sidelines.

'I'm amazed at the response from my friends and family to be honest with you,' he says. 'They all love it.

'This show brings such a lot of pleasure to viewers. Being invited on the show is such a privilege and I don't want to waste that opportunity.'

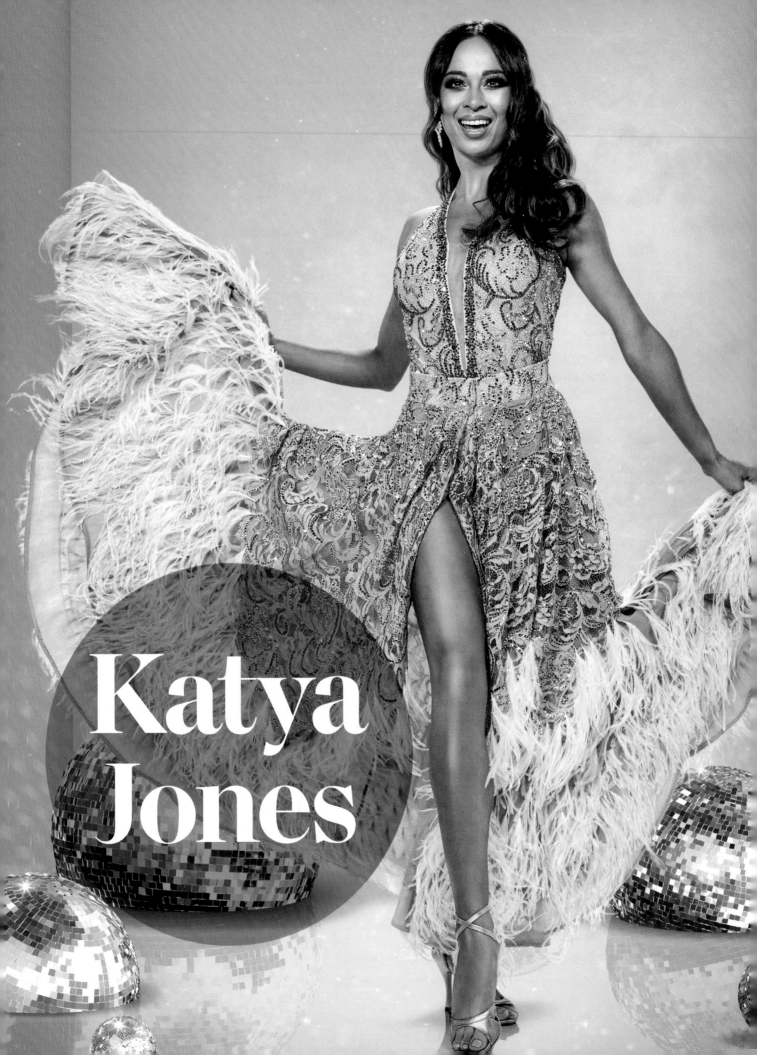

Katya Jones

Katya Jones has been paired with former footballer Tony Adams for this series of *Strictly* and she says he is already having a ball after his dance-floor debut at the launch show.

'Tony gives it a go. He's got rhythm and loves music,' she says. 'That's the main thing. It's hard to say how good he will be from the launch show's group dance, but I know he loved his first dance. He smiled all the way through, which is a good sign.'

Although he is a complete novice, Katya says her new partner has the makings of a dancer. And, as her third athlete in a row – after boxer Nicola Adams and swimmer Adam Peaty – she says the sporting mentality can be a bonus.

'Tony listens really well in rehearsal and he's an athlete, so he knows how to connect his brain to his body and to his muscles, so that's very promising,' she says.

While Tony has a cheeky sense of humour, Katya says he is taking the competition seriously.

'He's not just come here for a laugh,' she says. 'He does want to have fun, which is great, but of course he does want to dance properly. Tony jokes that he should have done it 20 years ago, but the discipline and mentality are still there. I also love that he has a lot of charisma, and that's something that you can't teach. You can bring it out, but he has it naturally, which is really cool to work with.

'Every single person is different and everyone has character, something about them, so what I love to do is to bring out their best and their fun side. But Tony is diving into it, fully committed.'

Katya began dancing at the age of six in her native St Petersburg and is three-time World Amateur Latin Champion. She won the World Professional Latin Showdance Championship in 2015 and is also the four-time undefeated British National Professional Champion. She made an unforgettable *Strictly* debut in series 14, dancing with Ed Balls, and she waltzed to victory with actor Joe McFadden a year later. Last year, she partnered Olympic gold medallist Adam Peaty, and says he was a model pupil.

'Sports people are always very focused and disciplined,' she says. 'They're used to being coached, they're used to being taught. It's an exciting thing to say that you've coached an Olympic champion – even if it's not in their discipline.'

As well as competing on the show, Katya danced in both the *Strictly Come Dancing Live!* tour and *Strictly Come Dancing: The Professionals* tour, and loved meeting fans around the country.

'There's nothing like the atmosphere of the arena tour. I remember finishing the very last show and, in the final dance, the dancers would lie on the stage. I had my eyes closed so I couldn't see the audience, but I could hear the huge roar. Moments like that are absolutely priceless. Just taking it all in and capturing that moment was awesome. It's so incredible to go around the country seeing the fans, making them happy – that's what *Strictly* does best. It brings joy. Whether it's the live tour, the pro tour or the Saturday-night show, it leaves everyone with a smile and brings the mood up.'

This year Katya is looking forward to the themed week and one very special *Strictly* venue.

'I always love Movie Week because of the storytelling and, for the first time, the celebs get to play a character and dress up,' she says. 'And I'm really looking forward to Blackpool Week because the group numbers are bigger, with extra dancers, and it's an incredible experience for the celebs to dance in the iconic Tower Ballroom. Making it to Blackpool is a good incentive for our partners to do well, so hopefully we can make it.'

The Pod Squad

From Tess and Claudia to the competing couples, *Strictly* has created many a brilliant double act. And since 2019 another dynamic duo, Kim Winston and Joe Sugg, have kept superfans up to date with all the backstage gossip on *Strictly Come Dancing: The Official Podcast*.

As a former producer on the live show, Kim's encyclopaedic knowledge of all things *Strictly* combines with Joe's own experience as a finalist to provide a unique insight into what goes on behind the scenes.

'I've done almost every job backstage so we try and give listeners two different perspectives, looking at how the show is made but also from the point of view of someone who has been a contestant himself,' explains Kim, who also produces the podcast. 'It worked well from the start because I learned from him and he learned from me. It's just the two of us – superfans for different reasons – having a good old natter about the show, getting interviews and asking questions that no one else has got access to, because we're able to be there behind the scenes. We just want it to be fun for the listeners.'

For YouTuber Joe, who was partnered with Dianne Buswell in series 16, taking part in *Strictly* was a life-changing experience.

'I really enjoyed *Strictly*,' he says. 'I'd never danced before so I was worried I would have two left feet, and it didn't come naturally, but luckily I picked it up pretty quick. As soon as that first week was over, I wanted to make sure I got to that Final.

'Before *Strictly* the thought of dancing on national television in front of 12 million people each week was daunting, and being on stage, dancing and singing, is something I'd never seen myself doing. But *Strictly* gave me such a big boost in confidence in myself and made me think you've just got to take these opportunities. Make the most of them and have fun with it.'

The social-media star has precious memories of his night in Blackpool and one very special guest.

'We performed a Quickstep to "Dancin' Fool", and I was really excited because it was the perfect fit for Blackpool,' he recalls. 'I got to wear the full tails and have the Fred Astaire haircut, so I felt like I'd gone back in time, to what it must have been like to dance in the Tower Ballroom. My family were in the audience and my nan, who's in her nineties and danced there herself in her younger days, travelled all the way up from Wiltshire. That was the first night I got three 10s so it was such a special evening.'

For Kim, who worked on the show from 2009, knowing the corridors and gallery at Elstree Studios like the back of her hand gives her a great advantage as a roving reporter.

'We're allowed access to every single corridor, every room and every person who works behind the scenes, from hair and make-up, costume and runners to the directors and the sound team in the gallery,' she says. 'We get bits of info like whose costume is being altered two hours before the show, what hair and make-up is planned and who's wearing a completely different look than they were in the dress rehearsal. We also see what the couples are like before a show. Some will have candles and Zen music, whereas others are having a disco with full-on music blaring.'

The podcast, which is recorded on the day of the live shows and released just hours later, features chats with the couples, the 'J Word' quiz

and listeners' questions for the *Strictly* stars each week. Craig Revel Horwood recently admitted he keeps a stash of sweets under his desk and Motsi Mabuse revealed she would have been a lawyer or politician if she hadn't been a dancer.

'We have learned that Motsi likes a party before the show with very loud music and Craig likes a nap,' Kim says. 'Shirley will only eat chicken on the day and Anton refuses to stay in his dressing room. He loves to be among the buzz because he was a pro for so many years, so while the other judges are in their rooms, he'll be wandering around downstairs. Also, if ever you've lost Katya, she's in wardrobe helping the team sew or stick on crystals at the last minute.'

The co-presenters didn't know each other before taking on the project and their first recording for the podcast was the opening show of 2019, when Kylie Minogue brought the house down.

'We had a quick podcast photoshoot and then it was straight into interviewing the celebrities and the pros, but straight away I clicked with Kim,' says Joe. 'We work really well as a team and she makes it an absolute joy.'

Kim is equally taken with Joe, calling him 'genuinely the nicest person'.

'I feel a bit like a big sister to Joe, because I'm a little older, but he's so much fun,' she adds. 'We get on really well, I think because he loves the show as much as I do. We are constantly texting each other during the week, chatting and gossiping about what's going on. We watch every *It Takes Two*, all the pros' and celebrities' social media, so we chat about those and when we get to Saturday you can't keep us quiet!'

'*Strictly* is escapism for a couple of hours a week and it spreads joy,' says Kim. 'That's down to the talent on screen but also behind the screen as well. Every year is brilliant and every year is my favourite, but 2021 will be a tough year to beat.'

Looking forward, Kim loves the build-up to each series, when the celebrities begin to be revealed.

'Joe and I get so excited when that first person is announced,' she says. 'We start frantically texting each other because we don't know in advance, so they're surprises for us as well, which I really like.

'You never know what journey people are going to go on, but we always try and guess who will be in the Final. It's really interesting looking back and seeing when we got it completely wrong, because that's the beauty of *Strictly*. You just don't know what's going to come.'

Joe is also excited about the cast announcements, as well as guessing who will be partnered with which pro.

'I look forward to the pro numbers as well because they're always brilliant and Jason Gilkison does a magnificent job on the choreography, coming up with new and interesting concepts each year and pushing the boundaries. I like watching the AR [augmented reality] technology, which gets better every year. I look forward to Craig giving that first 10 of the series and this year I'm looking forward to Anton being back on the judges' desk, because he is hilarious. But most of all I'm looking forward to working with Kim again, because she's amazing!'

Strictly Come Dancing: The Official Podcast is available on BBC Sounds. BBC Sounds can be found online or as a mobile app.

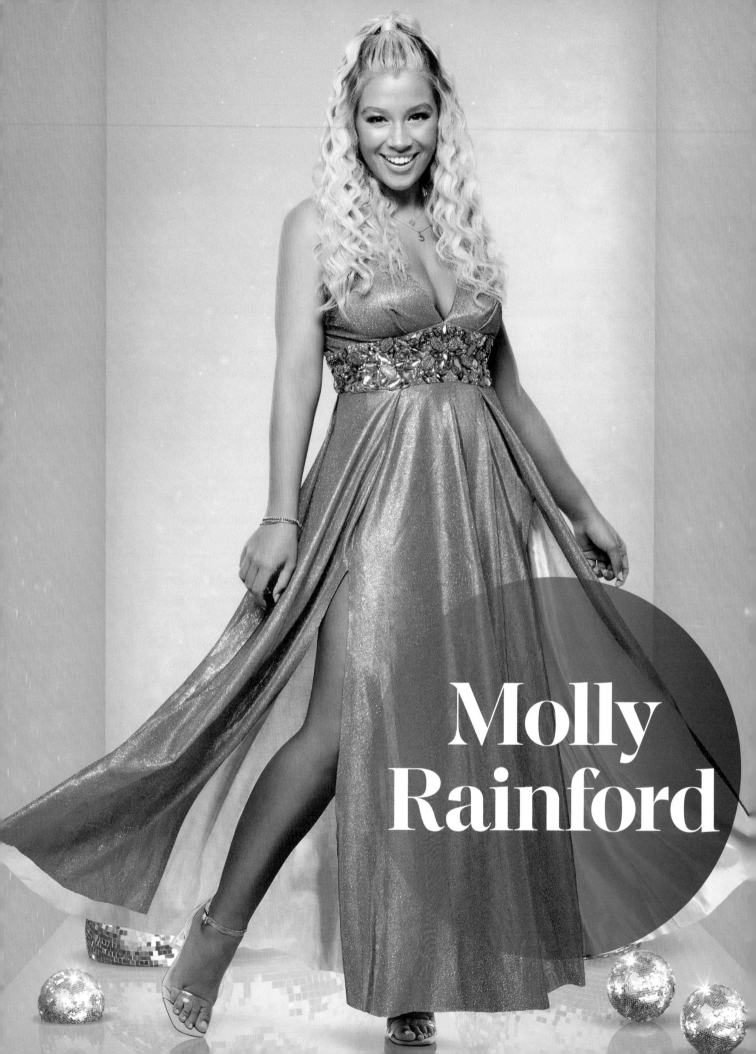

Molly
Rainford

As TV's Nova Jones, a galactic pop star, Molly Rainford has a huge fanbase of younger viewers. And as an avid fan of *Strictly*, she is hoping many of her followers will tune in to watch her on the dance floor.

'I'm really excited to be on *Strictly* because it's such a family show,' she says. 'I've been watching it since I was little with my family. There are so many people that I know my nan will recognise and my mum will recognise, so there's something for all the family, and I think that's the beauty of it. Hopefully, kids will see me and recognise me – although I look a little bit different to my character because I always wear wigs for the part.'

Her fictional alter ego is no stranger to glitter and sparkle, dressing in elaborate space-age costumes for her performances, so Molly will feel right at home in *Strictly*'s costume department.

'I'm buzzing for the costumes, but they'd be casual for Nova Jones!' she says. 'It's going to be nice to do it as me, as Molly, rather than a character, and see what that looks like.'

Molly first sprang to fame at the age of 11, when she reached the 2012 final of *Britain's Got Talent* and landed a recording contract. She went on to present *Friday Download* on CBBC before landing the role of space-travelling singer Nova in 2021. Now she's hoping her musical talent and acting skills will help her on the *Strictly* floor.

'I hope those skills will translate,' she says. 'Because I sing, I do have that bit of musicality and rhythm, so I get the count on the beat. I don't know if it's going to translate to my feet, but that's what I'm here for. With the acting, I know expression is important, and I'm told that as long as you look like you're having fun, the audience will have fun with you.'

Molly, who hails from Essex, is paired with new arrival Carlos Gu and says she's looking forward to being his debut dancing partner. 'For me, this is a really special experience because it's not just my first *Strictly*, but it's Carlos's as well,' she says. 'It's going to be really amazing going through that together and we'll always have that – "I was your first partner and you were mine." There's a bit of pressure, too, because I want to be a good partner and not let him down, but it's an exciting partnership for me.'

The talented singer is used to performing and says dancing in front of millions of viewers will be 'nerve-wracking but really exciting'.

'There are so many people watching at home, so to stop me getting nervous I'm going to focus on the people in the room,' she says. 'I've already bonded so well with the other contestants and it's all about supporting each other. I am looking forward to having my family there too.'

As this year's youngest contestant, at 21, Molly says, 'There's a bit of pressure for me to have good stamina, but I don't know if that's the case.'

But while she's not eyeing up the competition, because she wants to focus on the task in hand, she has got the glitterball trophy in her sights.

'You can't come into *Strictly* and not have your eyes on the prize a little bit!' she says. 'I'm definitely going to be giving it my all. I want to give it a good go and hopefully get there.'

Carlos Gu

Until July, Carlos Gu was still competing on the International Championship circuit – *Strictly Come Dancing* is his first foray into television. Even so, it wasn't until he got into the rehearsal room that it all hit home.

'It's an amazing feeling, joining *Strictly*, and I'm beyond happy,' he says. 'When I got the call I was quite calm because I had some sort of instinct. I knew it was going to happen, because this is my goal. Also, it was a long-distance call, so while you hear it, you don't physically feel it, see it or touch it. But when I physically arrived in London to join the rehearsal, the first week was blowing my mind. Being in the rehearsal studio was the moment I felt like, "Wow, I'm finally joining *Strictly*. This is the dream come true!"

'The launch show was also a big event for me. To see all the dancers and celebs and everybody involved in the show was amazing. They have all been so warm and made me feel at home, so I'm thrilled to be here.'

Born in Taiyuan, China, Carlos started dancing at the age of 11, encouraged by his mum.

'I've always been very energetic and I can't stay still,' he explains. 'As soon as I heard music I was moving. So my mum sent me to my first dance school and I started to learn Latin dance.'

Carlos went on to become Chinese National Latin Champion and Asian Champion. The dancer's family were delighted when he was offered the show.

'My mum is especially very happy because she knew living in England has always been one of my dreams,' he says.

Partnered with singer and actress Molly Rainford, Carlos is delighted with progress so far.

'Wow, I'm so lucky to get Molly in my first year. She has everything needed to be a good dancer. She has rhythm, and she is learning so fast. Her musical ear helps. I'm really looking forward to seeing what she can do.'

Coming straight from the more rigidly judged competition world, Carlos is also relishing the chance to be more creative and expressive in his choreography.

'Even though it's all about ballroom and Latin dance, it is completely different when it comes to the level of the performance and entertainment and also the level of presentation,' he says. 'Competition is stricter. Dancing on the show still requires rules and discipline, but it's more open; we have more choices and more chance to express ourselves.'

As a competitor, Carlos has danced at Blackpool for the last 10 years and is keen to get back there this year with Molly.

'It will be a very different experience, but Blackpool is where the dream started for every dancer,' he says. 'So I'm very happy that I'll be going back to dance there because I missed it this year.'

Being as new to the *Strictly* floor as his partner will also be a help rather than a hindrance, according to Carlos.

'I think the series being a first for both of us is our advantage because we are fresh, we're excited about it and we can bring a lot of high energy to the routines,' he says.

'It's my first year and what I want to do is just enjoy it as much as possible and to make a really good show that people will remember. I want to make an impact on the dance floor.'

Tess Daly

As the iconic *Strictly* theme strikes up and the celebrities and pros gather for a sparkling new series, host Tess Daly is brimming with anticipation for the weeks ahead.

'I have high hopes for this year,' she says. 'It's our twentieth series and it already feels like it's fizzing with excitement.'

Having watched the launch-show group dance and passed an experienced eye over the talent, Tess is impressed with the new crop and has spotted potential.

'It was exciting because the group dance is the first time you see the celebrities on the dance floor,' she says. 'There are some seriously good dancers this year. They can move – and all of them looked great. There's a lot of talent there so it's going to be an exciting competition.'

As host of the live shows since day one, Tess has seen hundreds of *Strictly* hopefuls take to the floor since 2004 and believes the recipe for success is hard work and commitment.

'My advice is to bring your heart to the dance floor because the more you give, the more we will love you for it. The competitiveness they start to feel after the first couple of weeks takes a lot of our celebrities by surprise. At first it's all fun and games, then they realise they really want to be good and need to work hard, so they get swept away in the *Strictly* bubble. I would say throw yourself into it 100 per cent and you'll have the time of your life.'

As well as watching the celebrities' progress each week, Tess is looking forward to Blackpool and the themed week in celebration of the BBC's centenary.

'The BBC special will be fun,' she says. 'There'll be a lovely nostalgic feel to the show and an air of celebration of a century of broadcasting.'

'Blackpool is my favourite show, bar the Final. It feels like a school trip when we decamp there for a couple of nights. You can't beat the Tower Ballroom for sheer ambience and the history of the place, and the audience is tripled. There's always a huge sense of anticipation as the live show starts and it feels like a huge event.'

Having worked alongside Anton Du Beke since the first show, Tess says her fellow *Strictly* stalwart proved a brilliant judge in the last series.

'Anton is so at home in his new role of judge; he brings a unique perspective because he's been on the other side of the judges' desk and he knows what the competitors are going through. He brings such warmth, empathy and great humour to the panel. He's been there since day one, like myself and Craig, and I love him to bits.'

As we head into series 20, Tess is delighted that the show's fan base has continued to grow, with viewers of all generations tuning in every weekend.

'We never take it for granted that our audience will come back year after year, and it's a huge privilege that they do and that they enjoy the show as much as they ever have,' she says. 'Our original audience is now watching with their children and their children's children. People tell me they've grown up watching the show and it's been a part of their Saturday night for as long as they can remember.

'It's feelgood television at its very best and it's so uplifting. So many people tell me they look forward to it coming back year after year and they don't mind that the winter nights are creeping in because it means *Strictly* is back on the telly. You can't underestimate how much that means in people's lives.

'Our only agenda is joy. It genuinely feels like an honour to have been part of that for the best part of two decades.'

Richie
Anderson

When the show kicked off last year Richie Anderson was throwing his annual *Strictly* launch party, immersing himself in the action. Now the Radio 2 presenter can't believe he'll be taking to the hallowed *Strictly* floor himself.

'I feel like I've won the top prize in a raffle!' he says. 'I love this show. Every year I have a launch party in my kitchen with my family and friends.

'I've been to three of the arena tours and was in the second row for one, which was amazing. I've been an audience guest on *It Takes Two* twice. This year I just wanted to get tickets to be in the studio audience and I've actually ended up as a dancer on the show. It's the best upgrade ever!'

While Richie is bubbling with excitement, his family are also over the moon that he's on the show.

'It means the world to my mum and my auntie Jacqui, who are *Strictly* superfans,' he says. 'Every *Strictly* night they call each othrer and have a little debrief, saying things like, "Seven? It should have been an eight!" My mum took Salsa lessons in 2014 and she thinks she's Shirley Ballas! She's already giving me tips and advice. They're so excited to come down to watch, and it will be amazing to dance when they're in the audience. Mum's the biggest Wham! fan and wants me to dance to one of their tracks, but I don't know if it's like a disco where you can make requests!'

Since 2019, Richie has been the travel announcer on the Radio 2 breakfast show with Zoe Ball, and he says the former finalist and *It Takes Two* presenter has been passing on a few tips.

'Zoe's given me a couple of dance lessons in the studio,' he says. 'When the songs are on she tells me, "This could be a Jive," or "This could be a Cha-cha-cha." We tried a few steps, then she said, "I'll leave it to your professional. There's a lot of work needs doing." But Zoe's great because she's obviously been through the process, and she's given me lots of words of encouragement. It's nice that I've got that support every day at work.'

Paired with Giovanni Pernice, Richie says he was inspired by watching John Whaite and Johannes Radebe's triumphant performances on the last series.

'Watching John and Johannes gave me the confidence to be in an all-male partnership this year,' he says. 'I'm so glad I'm doing it. I just felt so much inspiration. I wish I could have seen that on TV when I was growing up as a teenager.'

Richie's signature moves are 'shimmy, body pop and a cartwheel', but he says apart from dancing club at the age of seven, he has had no formal training. Now he's hoping Giovanni, who lifted the glitterball last year with Rose Ayling-Ellis, can remedy that.

'Giovanni is an incredible teacher and such a nice guy,' he says. 'I've watched him and Rose do their Couple's Choice dance about a million times and never without crying, so I'm excited to be dancing with him. But I move a bit like a folded-up ironing board so let's see how he gets on with that!'

Giovanni Pernice

Reigning

champion Giovanni Pernice stormed to victory last year, winning the hearts of the nation with actress Rose Ayling-Ellis. This year he is dancing in an all-male pairing with radio presenter Richie Anderson, and he is relishing the new challenge.

'It's going to be different again because obviously there's a leader and a follower, and being an all-male pairing means we can swap around,' he says. 'I used to teach same-sex couples, as we all do in our dance careers, so it's something we are all familiar with.

'Richie is doing pretty well, but he has not come from a pop background and has no dance experience. What he does have is plenty of sass and energy. If you could bottle his energy and sell it, we'd be rich!'

The couple kicked off with a Cha-cha-cha, which suits Richie's energetic style, but Giovanni says he may have to rein him in a little for the slower dances. 'He's got so much energy,' he jokes. 'He is so bouncy!'

As a *Strictly* superfan, Richie has a wealth of knowledge when it comes to the dances and is throwing himself into the routines.

'Richie's been watching for a long time so he knows what a straight leg means and what Craig wants to see in certain dances,' says Giovanni. 'But there's a difference between studying and dancing. You might know what the judges want, but you have to translate those moves to your own body, which is not easy.'

As Richie is immersing himself in the experience, Giovanni has a few surprises lined up – especially in the themed weeks.

'I love Movie Week and Musicals Week because you can dress up, and because Richie is a character, I think I can throw everything at him that I've wanted to do in the past and he'll say, "That's fine. That's cool." I'm looking forward to that.'

Born in Sicily, Giovanni left home at 14 to study dance in Bologna and began competing as an adult in 2008. Four years later, he was crowned Italian Champion and he went on to compete in numerous international contests. He joined *Strictly* in 2015 and, after Final appearances with Georgia May Foote, Debbie McGee and Faye Tozer, he finally lifted the prize with Rose last year.

'The whole series was magical, and it wasn't just about the glitterball, it was about what we achieved along the way,' he says. 'We raised awareness for the deaf community, so it was much more than just the competition for me and Rose; it felt like an unbelievable accomplishment and a fantastic journey. It was so special.'

'We had to be facing each other throughout because Rose was following by lip reading, watching my body language and counting, so that changed the way I choreographed. But Rose and I had a fantastic connection and she could understand me by just looking in my eyes. We clicked straight away and it's one of those once-in-a-lifetime relationships. We'll be friends forever.'

Rose's Couple's Choice, when the music stopped and they danced in silence, brought the nation to tears, and Giovanni says he's proud of its dramatic impact.

'I wanted to show the audience what Rose was feeling every week, what she was going through and how she was dancing without hearing the music. I think we achieved that, and we ended up winning a BAFTA, which was amazing.

'For the launch show, we danced our Viennese Waltz, which incorporated British Sign Language into the movements. The first time we danced it online searches for BSL increased 2,000 per cent … So we achieved a few things, looking back.'

Having finally got his hands on the coveted glitterball trophy, Giovanni handed it over to his biggest fans, his parents.

Guess the Dance

Do you know your Samba from your Rumba? Can you tell an Argentine Tango from an American Smooth? Below are pictures of iconic dances from the *Strictly* archives. All you have to do is remember which dance each couple was performing at the time.

Answers on p128

1

Zero to Hero
Jamie Laing and Karen Hauer definitely put the glad in gladiator with their Hercules routine in the series-18 Final. But what was the dance?

2

Most Wanted
This week-three marvel was voted the most memorable *Strictly* dance of all time in a 2020 poll. But what were The Wanted star Jay McGuiness and Aliona Vilani performing?

3

Mag-nificent
Dancing to 'Magalenha', Oti Mabuse and Danny Mac reached the record books after being awarded the first perfect score on the show for which dance style?

Styling It Out
Former Shadow Chancellor Ed Balls's 'Gangnam Style' routine with Katya Jones went down in history. But which Latin dance was it?

Swing Vote
AJ Odudu and Kai Widdrington were the only series-19 couple to score a perfect 40 for this ballroom dance, which they performed to Benny Goodman's 'Sing, Sing, Sing'. What was it?

Final Triumph
Debbie McGee and Giovanni Pernice blew the judges away with which elegant dance?

Raining Supreme

Presenter Ore Oduba and partner Joanne Clifton splashed their way to victory with their Movie Week routine to 'Singin' in the Rain'. But which ballroom dance was it?

8

Wild Woman

Anton Du Beke wiped the floor with former MP Ann Widdecombe in this memorable Halloween Week number to The Troggs' 'Wild Thing'. But what dance were they performing?

Kym
Marsh

As a presenter on *Morning Live*, Kym Marsh has taken part in a few *Strictly* workouts with the show's pros, but gearing up for the real thing has meant upping her fitness regime.

'I'm someone who generally likes to go to the gym, but I was plagued with quite a lot of injuries last year, and this is probably the worst shape I've been in for the last five years,' she says. 'My exercise regime has not been as good as it would normally be, but I ran the Manchester 10k in May, so that was the beginning of my journey. Since I agreed to do *Strictly*, I've been getting back in the gym. My husband's in the military and he's really helpful and helps me train quite a lot.'

The singer, actress and presenter has been keen to take on *Strictly* for a while but says there was a very moving reason why she said yes to the challenge this year.

'My dad has been unwell and over the years he's told me, "You never know what's around the corner, so grab the chances in life and do it." Then he was diagnosed with incurable cancer last March, so I'm trying to do everything I can while he's here, so he can join in and be part of it.

'Also, my husband is home at the moment, so he can come and watch and cheer me on, but next year he might be off on tour somewhere, so I thought now is the time to grab the opportunity while I can.'

Manchester-born Kym was put together with four bandmates to form Hear'Say after auditioning as a solo act on *Popstars* in 2000. The band broke chart records with their first single, 'Pure and Simple', which sold 550,000 copies, and followed up with a hit album, *Popstars*, but Kym left in 2002 to pursue a solo career. After a stint on *Loose Women*, Kym joined *Coronation Street* and spent 13 years playing Michelle Connor before leaving in 2019. She now stars in school drama *Waterloo Road* as well as presenting BBC magazine programme *Morning Live*, where she has already got to know dance partner Graziano Di Prima.

'I'm very fortunate that I knew Graziano a little bit before this and he's a genuinely nice guy,' she says. 'He wants to teach, he wants me to learn, and I know that he's going to work me, but he's also patient and kind. He gives you praise too and I think that's important. I'm also hoping we'll have a bit of a laugh along the way.'

'During my time with Hear'Say, I found the dance element really hard,' she says. 'We went on tour and doing all the dance routines for that was tricky! The choreographer used to laugh at me because I would always say, "I can't do it." I was in *Saturday Night Fever* for six months in the West End too, but I had a part that required little dancing, and that was kind of on purpose.'

The former soap star is 'very excited' about putting on the glitz for the show.

'I'm really looking forward to it and I think that's one of the great things about *Strictly*, apart from obviously the dancing and how wonderful that is,' she says. 'The glamour and the glitz are always going to be something that people love, and I'll definitely enjoy that side of it. The first time we got in the costumes and make-up as a trial run was amazing and it does make you feel the part.'

Graziano
Di Prima

Sicilian

Sicilian dancer Graziano Di Prima had already put partner Kym Marsh through her paces in the *Strictly* fitness workouts on *Morning Live* before they were paired up. But he says learning a whole routine will prove a bit more difficult.

'I'm over the moon to have Kym as a partner,' he says. 'I used to see her when I did the *Morning Live* fitness slot and I would think, "Why has she never been on *Strictly*? She could be really good." So I was ecstatic when we were paired up. We danced well together as part of the group dance on the launch show.

'She is working so hard and doing really well. On her second day of training we almost finished the whole routine, which is great progress.'

The pair started their *Strictly* journey with a fast and furious Jive, dubbed the Morning Jive by the couple, and Graziano thinks the presenter has what it takes to keep the momentum up.

'The Jive is very quick, a very difficult one to learn, but Kym is very precise, wanting to do everything perfectly,' he says. 'She's got musicality, she's an actress so she knows how to portray a part. I don't need to say, "Let's do that again" because she wants to do better herself.

'Also, she is a massive fan of the show and knows everything about it. She can't wait to enjoy this process and she really wants to put the hours in. She's giving me everything she's got.'

As a teacher Graziano says, 'I like to push my celebrity a little to get the best out of them.'

Graziano took up dancing at six in his native Sicily and, at 17, he moved to Bologna to compete. He went on to become Italian Latin Champion and has also represented Belgium at the World Championships. He joined *Strictly* in 2018, dancing with DJ Vick Hope. Graziano holds the Guinness World Record for the most Botafogo dance steps in 30 seconds, with a total of 90, achieved on *It Takes Two*. Last year, he shook up the floor with comedian Judi Love.

'Judi was amazing and she's a friend for life,' he says. 'She trained with me from 10 to 6, non-stop. She really pushed herself and we had the best time together. We laughed so much. She is genuinely the most hilarious person I ever met in my life.'

The couple's Samba, to Sean Paul's 'Get Busy', was a sensation and Graziano's favourite dance of the series.

'The Samba was iconic,' he says. 'Judi told me, "This dance is going to have proper Jamaican movements," and she put in some great moves. It was an amazing surprise when Sean Paul sent in a video saying he loved the routine. I was over the moon.'

Graziano has had a busy year so far. As well as getting married to fiancée Giadi Lini, he performed in both the *Strictly* arena tour and the *Professionals* tour.

'My wedding was the best day of my life – we finally had the chance to get married in my hometown in Sicily, in a castle by the beach. It was beautiful,' he says.

'I also had the best time on the pro tour and dancing the arena tour. It was brilliant touring with the group and we had so much fun. The audience was incredible. Everything about *Strictly*, from the audience, the production down to the catering, is perfect.'

Now looking forward to a new series, Graziano says he had a blast at the launch show and is excited for the weeks ahead.

Word Search

Are your eagle eyes as good as your twinkle toes? See if you can spot all 16 answers in our wickedly wonderful word search.

Answers on p126

C	B	A	E	S	M	G	R	I	O	I	N	K	B	N
H	H	D	A	V	E	A	R	C	H	O	R	C	L	E
R	R	J	O	L	L	C	E	K	S	E	I	V	A	D
E	G	V	D	S	A	N	C	N	H	D	M	I	O	D
V	U	S	Y	Y	E	C	A	T	S	A	A	E	P	A
A	Q	W	W	A	D	M	F	R	O	Y	X	N	O	F
K	T	S	A	N	E	L	L	B	P	Z	N	N	C	C
E	X	I	O	L	Y	X	V	A	A	N	E	E	L	M
J	E	T	K	A	T	A	A	I	D	A	W	S	O	E
L	T	N	Z	I	Y	Z	Y	L	D	X	Y	E	P	O
A	I	L	W	T	N	A	V	E	L	Z	O	O	E	J
W	O	S	A	L	L	A	B	Y	E	L	R	I	H	S
Y	O	K	R	A	G	E	X	S	H	I	K	L	Y	A
I	J	V	I	E	N	E	W	Y	C	R	E	P	P	X
D	U	B	E	O	R	C	H	E	S	T	R	A	R	C

Claudia's surname (9)

Classic ballroom dance (5)

Twirlier version of the above (8)

Nina -----, series-19 contestant (5)

Head judge (7, 6)

Dance step named after residents of the Big Apple (3, 6)

What the judges hold up after a dance (6)

Bill ------, series-18 champ (6)

Strictly's music maestro (4, 4)

Led by the clue above, they provide the live music (9)

Actor and series-15 winner (3, 8)

First name of the pro who took the trophy with the above (5)

Former champ Ms Dooley (6)

Singer who made it to the Final with Janette Manrara in series 18 (4)

First name of the dancer who made his debut with Tilly Ramsay (6)

Series-19 Dragon, Sara (6)

Crossword

A *Strictly* teatime teaser to get the grey cells tingling.

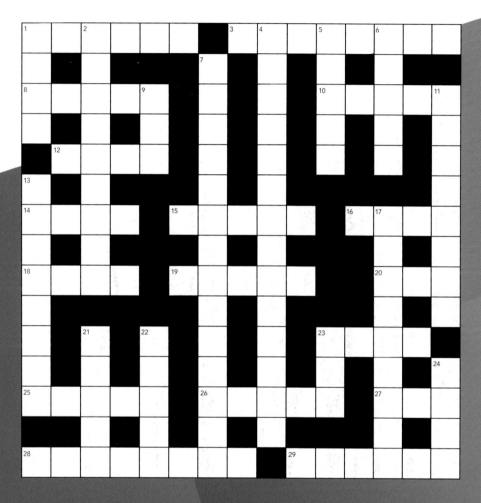

Answers on p127

Across

1. & 13 Down. Series 17 *Strictly* champion (6, 8)
3. See 1 Down
8. Dance that originated in Buenos Aires (5)
10. Shirley Ballas was known as the Queen of this (5)
12. Surname of Lee, Blue singer and former *Strictly* contestant (4)
14. Joe Sugg did his showdance to the track 'I Bet You – – – – Good on the Dance Floor' (4)
15. Gabby – – – – –, sports presenter who competed in series five (5)
16. '– – – – a Feeling', *Flashdance* song chosen for Denise Van Outen's showdance (4)
18. Ms Daly (4)
19. Dance move with arms swinging from side to side at the back and front of the body, popular in 2017 (5)
20. Alex Scott danced a Paso Doble in Blackpool to Beyoncé's '– – – the World (Girls)' (3)
23. First name of Ms Tozer, series-16 finalist (4)
25. The dance of love (5)
26. Judge, Mr Du Beke (5)
27. First name of series-19 contestant, Mr Monye (3)
28. A girl's best friend, according to Marilyn Monroe (8)
29. Could be hair accessories used by *Strictly* stylists or dance movements to the side while keeping contact with the floor (6)

Down

1. & 3 Across. *Good Morning Britain* presenter who danced with Anton Du Beke in series five (4, 8)
2. American Jive-like dances occasionally featured in the show in the past (5, 4)
4. Ballroom-based dance influenced by the musicals of Hollywood's golden age (8, 6)
5. Surname of both a *Countdown* queen and an *Emmerdale* star who have competed in the show (5)
6. The pros danced in tanks of this for a group dance to 'Here Comes the Rain Again' and 'Umbrella' (5)
7. South African dancer who is now the youngest *Strictly* pro (7, 7)
9. Clara Amfo danced a Viennese Waltz to the Lesley Gore track 'You Don't – – – Me' (3)
11. '– – – – – / – – – Day', Cole Porter song Jamie Laing danced to in series 18 (5, 3)
13. See 1 Across
17. Series-nine winner (5, 4)
21. Latin party dance (5)
22. Instrument that comes in Grand or Upright and is often played by Dave Arch (5)
23. An avid viewer of *Strictly* (3)
24. 'The – – – –', Diana Ross song Sara Davies danced a Cha-cha-cha to in series 19 (4)

Will Mellor

Actor

Will Mellor is known for numerous TV roles, from lads' lad Gaz in *Two Pints of Lager and a Packet of Crisps* to evil villain Harvey in *Coronation Street*. Now the star says he's ready to take on the role of ballroom dancer in memory of his late dad, who passed away in 2020.

'I never saw myself doing *Strictly* because I was scared of stepping out of my comfort zone and I was overthinking things when it came to my acting career,' he says. 'Then I lost my dad and everything changed. I realised what life's about and that's grabbing opportunities and making memories, so I decided to say yes to more experiences. So this came along at the right time.

'It's my mum's favourite show and she's had a terrible few years losing my dad, her brother, brother-in-law and sister-in-law, so it's been a really tough time. But this has given her something to look forward to, so we are on this journey together, to create some fun and create memories.'

The Mancunian began acting as a teenager, starring in *Children's Ward*, before going on to regular roles in *Hollyoaks*, *Casualty* and the comedy *Two Pints of Lager* ..., which ran for 10 years. He has also starred in *Waterloo Road*, *White Van Man* and *Broadchurch*, and earlier this year fronted a dramatic storyline as gang leader Harvey Gaskell in *Corrie*.

A keen amateur boxer in the past, Will has been heading to the gym in preparation for his stint on *Strictly*, but he says, 'The problem is, I don't bend. I used to box and I do weights, but I'm not going to go into this thinking I'm ready, because I'm not. I've been ticking over in the gym, trying to keep my fitness up to a certain extent.

'I'm looking forward to doing something that's out of my comfort zone. With actors, costumes really do help you feel the part so I'm hoping when I get the gear on I'll feel great.'

Will admits that the first training session, for the launch show, came as a shock, but he loved the camaraderie of training alongside his fellow celebs.

'The first dance, I thought we'd walk on, twirl about a bit and walk off,' he laughs. 'But in the first rehearsals my legs took over my body. I looked down and thought, "They can't be my legs." It was great for us all to be together and we had loads of fun getting to know each other.'

Paired with Nancy Xu, Will says he is ready to knuckle down to produce the best dance possible.

'I was pleased when I was partnered with her,' he says. 'Nancy is great. We've both got high energy and she's an amazing dancer, as they all are. She's perfect for me because I don't take myself that seriously, but I am going to take the dancing seriously and I want to enjoy this journey and go as far as we can go with it.'

While Will has his eye on the prize, his first benchmark is making it to Blackpool – although not necessarily as a contestant.

'I've decided I'm going to Blackpool anyway,' he jokes. 'If I'm not through, I'll do the Pleasure Beach and watch the show with a stick of rock in my hand and a kiss-me-quick hat!'

Nancy Xu

After an amazing debut in the couples' competition last year with Rhys Stephenson, Nancy Xu is back for more *Strictly* fun. This time she'll be putting actor Will Mellor through his paces.

'Will is amazing, I like him very much,' she says. 'Every time we are at rehearsal, he gives it 100 per cent. He will say to me, "Are you happy with where we are now? If you are happy then I am happy, and if not, we'll keep going." But I know he has already given me everything and as a teacher I really appreciate that.'

'In the first week we were trying a bit of everything because we have to prepare. His movement is really good but that doesn't mean you can dance ballroom and Latin, because they have a very specific technique. Unless you have had experience before, you have learned a dance before, it is very difficult to pick up. Even for a ballet or contemporary dancer, coming back to Latin and ballroom is a totally different way to perform.'

Born in China, Nancy has competed all over the world and has numerous titles to her name, including runner-up at the 2013 International Singapore Championships, third place in the 2010–2012 CBDF National Amateur Latin Championships and finalist in the U21 World Championships in 2010. She joined *Strictly* in 2019 and last year she reached the Semi-finals with TV presenter Rhys.

'Rhys and I had a lovely time together. It was really a tough year, competition wise, and Rhys did so well to get to the Semi-finals, but he deserved it because he worked so hard.'

Among Nancy's favourite dances were their Quarter-final Argentine Tango and the week-eight Charleston, which earned them a perfect score.

'I really enjoyed our Spider-Man dance in Movie Week, too. We had a lovely week and it was so much fun.'

As well as dancing together in the *Strictly Come Dancing Live!* tour after the series ended, Nancy and Rhys have filmed some online content for kids, teaching them Nancy's native Mandarin. Nancy says her two *Strictly* partners have a lot in common when it comes to their approach to learning.

'Both Will and Rhys really want to do well and I appreciate that,' she says. 'I know it can be scary because they are trying to learn a difficult skill that they've never learned before. Despite that, they both give everything they can to show me what they can do and, as a dance teacher, that helps.

'They have to learn everything in a few days. It's a big challenge for them because the steps look easy, effortless, and it's only when you try them that you realise how hard they are. They both have remarkably similar musical tastes to me, which is a bonus because music is such a big part of the show. With both of them, I've been very lucky.'

After coming so close to the Final last year, Nancy now has her eye on the prize.

'Will has lots of ideas of his own and there's one special dance he wants to dedicate to his mum,' she says. 'I have told him I am not planning for him to do one show, I'm planning for us to be there to the end. We're going to make it happen.'

Rylan

For those fans who need an extra top-up of sparkles between the live shows, *It Takes Two* is there to keep fans up to date with all things *Strictly* throughout the week, and presenter Rylan is raring to go.

'I can't wait to get back in the studio,' he says. 'It's so nice to be back and I'm looking forward to giving everyone a big old cuddle. I'm really excited about this year's line-up and I can't wait to see how they all get on. Whenever the *Strictly* line-up is announced, everyone's got something to say and there's a real buzz. I met a couple of them at a photoshoot and they're all just so excited.'

When it comes to predicting who will make it through the final stages, Rylan is reserving judgement until the stars take to the floor.

'I might have my eye on one or two of them – although I couldn't reveal who!' he laughs. 'I normally do quite well with guesses, but I don't make any predictions until I've seen them in training. With *Strictly*, you don't know what people are going to be like or what abilities they have until it gets started. When you see them dance, it all changes.'

Although he has many favourite moments from last year, Rylan says the Final was one of the most memorable shows ever.

'The series last year was amazing and I loved watching John and Johannes, who absolutely smashed it,' he says. 'But one of my favourite moments, in a really strange way, was seeing AJ Odudu support everyone at the Final knowing she should have been up there, had she not been injured. It goes to show how close the cast gets during the show, and seeing her smiling and just happy to still be a part of it was a lovely moment.'

On *It Takes Two*, he is keen to brush up on his own dancing skills – which are improving year on year.

'Choreography Corner will be back and I love learning all the dances,' he says. 'But my favourite part is the Friday panel, and just having a bit of a gossip.'

Rylan, who is fronting the show on Mondays, Tuesdays and Fridays, will be sharing duties with former *Strictly* pro Janette Manrara for the second year. And he says his talented co-star smashed her debut as an *It Takes Two* presenter in the last series.

'Janette was an absolute breeze,' he says. 'She's part of the family anyway and she settled straight in. I think she did such an amazing job and it's so nice watching her fly. She's a dream to work with.'

Ellie Taylor

Comedian

Ellie Taylor says she and her mum are *Strictly* superfans and they're both 'over the moon' that she signed up to the show this year. But, while she jokes that she has 'the dancing ability of a newly born giraffe', she is taking the competition seriously.

'Graceful is not a word that would ever be applied to me, but I have lots of energy and a good work ethic,' she says. 'I would love to make it to Musicals Week, because I love musicals.'

After a brief stint in modelling, Ellie turned to stand-up in her mid-twenties and was discovered on the talent show *Show Me the Funny*. She has toured with five self-penned shows and been a regular on *Mock the Week*, as well as appearing on *8 Out of 10 Cats*, *The Mash Report* and *The Last Leg*. She has also had her own show on Heart FM and, in 2021, published her bestselling book *My Child and Other Mistakes*.

Ellie, who 'retired from tap and ballet lessons' at the age of seven, has no other dance experience and jokes that partner Johannes Radebe has his work cut out.

'My friends used to go off to dance class at Pineapple Dance Studios and they filmed it, but I couldn't think of anything worse than watching myself attempting to dance,' she laughs. 'During lockdown, I saw someone had done a dance workout online so I thought I'd try it, but I ended up stopping after five minutes and falling about laughing because I was so bad and so uncoordinated.'

The Essex-born comic has already bonded with Johannes and says he is the perfect partner to guide her through her *Strictly* journey.

'I'm really pleased I've got him, but I don't know how pleased he is to have me!' she jokes. 'When we first met, I told Johannes I work well with praise. I need pats on the head and someone to stroke my hand. I'm a bit of a baby so I just need someone to be like, "There, there. It will be okay."

'He knows that I'm coming from nothing and he's been really sweet and very patient. Plus he laughs a lot, which is great. He's such a giggler so we are having a lot of fun together.'

While she is looking forward to all the dances, Ellie says she is hoping to nail the ballroom frame once she gets in hold.

'I'd like to do the fun ones, like a Jive or a Charleston, but I would really like to learn some poise, to finally control my limbs,' she says. 'It would be lovely to do a great ballroom routine where I can look like an elegant lady.'

So, what will be Ellie's biggest challenge in the *Strictly* experience?

'All of it will be a challenge,' she says. 'I won't find wearing beautiful clothes and having lovely hair and make-up done a challenge – that will be an absolute pleasure. But everything else is very much out of my comfort zone!'

Ellie's parents, who have watched the show for years, will be cheering her on every step of the way.

'I don't think my parents have told their friends what I've been doing for ages,' she laughs. 'But they're really proud I'm doing this. My mum is delighted!'

Johannes Radebe

In series 19, Johannes Radebe made *Strictly* history with partner John Whaite, taking *Strictly*'s first all-male couple to the Final. Now, the former South African champion is paired with comedian Ellie Taylor and is hoping to make it all the way through again.

'So far it has been bliss,' he says. 'Ellie is a wonderful woman and makes going to work a joy. She's excited. Something magical happened in our first few days of rehearsal and she told me, "I was terrified, but I didn't know I was going to enjoy it this quickly." *Strictly* has already taken her over. She's thinking about it when she goes to sleep, when she's in the kitchen; she's showing her husband what she's learned.

'She was nervous about the group dance on the launch show, but once she had done it she said, "I want to do it again." That's the reaction I want. For me to see how invested she is as a non-dancer really humbles my heart.'

Starting their series with a Quickstep, Johannes says he hasn't tried her Latin skills yet.

'Ellie has never danced, so all of this is very new, and I can't wait to see how all the dances sit on her,' he says. 'I think her ballroom will be beautiful, although she doesn't consider herself elegant. She has surprised herself already and it's nice when she gets something right, because you can see the happiness and joy in her face.'

Having a comedian as a partner also means Johannes can have lots of fun, both on and off the dance floor.

'I have never laughed as much on *Strictly*, since day one of rehearsal, so it would be daft of me not to capitalise on that,' he says. 'I think putting some comedy into some of the routines will actually bring her comfort as well. After all, it's dancing. It should be fun!'

Born in Zamdela, Sasolburg, in South Africa, Johannes began dancing at seven, competing in provincial Latin competitions. He is two-time Professional South African Latin Champion and three-time South African Amateur Latin Champion. He joined the South African version of *Strictly Come Dancing* in 2014, twice making the Final.

In 2018, he joined the UK show and last year made it all the way to the Final.

'John was a fantastic dancer from the outset, but he didn't know his own potential,' he says. 'I pushed him because I saw what he could do and knew we were in for a fantastic series. It was lovely to have somebody that matched me in personality, who was as focused as I was throughout that journey. We understood each other and what we were there to do and it was beautiful.'

As an all-male pairing, Johannes and John were able to swap leads, meaning new possibilities in the choreography.

'I had never really danced in that role so it was a learning curve for me, while I was also busy trying to teach John. But I loved the dynamic of it all, the partnership, the chemistry and the strength. It added so much beauty to what is already beautiful in the ballroom and Latin worlds, and it said to people, there's nothing wrong in two beautiful bodies dancing to a piece of music. I think that will live on in people's minds.'

In the Final, the couple danced an unforgettable showdance as well as their *Pirates of the Caribbean* Paso Doble, scoring a perfect 40 for both.

'The Final felt surreal and very emotional,' says Johannes. 'It dawned on both of us that it was the last time we would dance on that *Strictly* floor and what this journey meant to us and so many people. It instilled a sense of confidence in both of us, to never shy away from who we are. When we took to the floor for the first dance, John thanked me for giving him a wonderful time, and for teaching him how to dance. I felt like a winner in that moment.'

This year, as always, Johannes wants to make sure his partner enjoys the *Strictly* experience.

'I want to have fun and give Ellie the best time of her life, because that's the most important thing,' he says. '*Strictly Come Dancing* has come a long way and it's part of our lives. It carries us through the winter months, and who doesn't love a little bit of sparkle, joy and escapism? I can't wait for all of it because I know that's how we connect with people at home. And what's more beautiful than that?'

Craig Revel Horwood

As *Strictly*'s longest-serving judge, Craig is an expert on the qualities that make a champion, and he has plenty of advice for the class of '22. As they take their first steps onto the floor, he reveals his recipe for a winning formula.

'It's hard work, dedication and wanting to win, primarily,' he says. 'You have to want the prize and it has to really mean something to you. The previous winners, including current champ Rose Ayling-Ellis, were hard workers, determined and they fell in love with the dancing, which is crucial.'

In terms of those all-important audience votes, the straight-talking judge believes giving fans a real glimpse of your character is key.

'Be honest and be yourself.,' he says. 'We want to get to know the celebrity for who they really are, not what they're famous for. Fans want to see the person behind the sports star, the actor or the presenter, and find out what really makes them tick.'

Having cast his eyes over the current crop, Craig says there is 'huge potential' among the contestants and he is hoping for a few surprises when they break out the moves.

'We've got such a good mix this year. There are actors, musicians, comedians, Olympians – they'll all bring the their professional experience and talents with them to the dance floor but we'll have to see how the cope with the challenges of the *Strictly* dance floor!'

This year sees the male-male pairing of Richie Anderson and Giovanni Pernice, but Craig says the dynamic is different to that of finalists John Whaite and Johannes Radebe.

'John and Johannes were amazing, but this is a different partnership altogether,' he says. 'You never know until they get on the floor and you see how the relationship develops. It's a far cry from radio presenting because you don't speak; you have to tell the story through movement. But Gio is a great teacher.'

With Anton Du Beke returning for his second year on the judges' panel, Craig admits the former *Strictly* pro is the perfect antidote to his own deadpan delivery.

'Judging is a perfect role for him and he is not afraid to show his emotional side, as we saw when he choked up over the unforgettable silent moment in Rose's Couple's Choice dance. Anton gets very emotional, and he lets the floodgates open, but that's good, because I'm the polar opposite!'

Craig is thrilled to be heading back up north for the mid-series special in Blackpool.

'It's going to be wonderful to return because of the electrifying atmosphere and the huge sprung dance floor. All the celebrities look forward to it because if they make it to Blackpool, they feel they've achieved something. It's a huge benchmark and after that you can see the potential winners and the battle's well and truly on.'

Looking back at the last series, Rose and Giovanni's iconic Contemporary routine was Craig's highlight, but he also loved the Grand Final, when the couple battled John and Johannes for the trophy.

'Both contestants were fantastic, so it really was neck and neck, which always makes a great Final. But it was a well-deserved win.'

As we go into the twentieth series, Craig, who was on board from the first show, jokes that one thing has made the show the huge success it is.

'It's Craig Revel Horwood, definitely,' he laughs. 'No, seriously, the success of the show is that it's won the hearts and minds of the nation. It gives fans something to believe in and gives them hope. And that's something we can all do with.'

Tyler West

DJ Tyler West is swapping his decks for the dance floor and says he will be cheered on by his delighted family, who are devoted fans of the show.

'My mum, aunt and nan have always watched *Strictly Come Dancing* religiously, and it's the thing my family all bond over,' he says. 'So when I told them I was coming on the show it all got a bit emotional. But then my mum was like, "Well, how are you going to do that?" But for me, when the offer came around, it was an absolute no-brainer. It's something I've always wanted to do and it's on my checklist of dream jobs for a TV and radio presenter.'

Paired with Dianne Buswell, Tyler says they already have a catchy team name. 'We're calling ourselves TyDi. We'll be bringing our merchandise soon,' he jokes. 'Dianne and I get on like a house on fire and she's like my sister. We just have so much banter and we get told off because we're like the naughty kids, laughing at the back.'

Londoner Tyler began his broadcasting career on CBBC before landing a presenting job on MTV at the age of 21. In 2019, he joined Kiss FM, where he hosts the weekday drive-time slot, and he also presents the BBC Three interior design show *Flat Out Fabulous* and *The MTV Movie Show*.

A keen music fan, the presenter has no dance training and says the ballroom hold could prove a challenge.

'Put me on a wedding dance floor and play Luther Vandross and I'm there,' he says. 'I'll do a nice little two-step or candy dance, but stepping onto the *Strictly* dance floor is a completely different ballgame. I might struggle with the ballroom posture. Dianne was telling me to imagine I've got tennis balls under my arms, make sure my chest is up, tape your fingers together to avoid spatula hands. I've got a lot to learn.'

When it comes to wardrobe, Tyler is ready to go for it.

'I'm game, 100 per cent,' he says. 'Get all the glitter over me and get me in all the outfits. We're putting on outfits that you'd never normally wear and that's great. But I don't like overheating so I avoid wearing too many items of clothing. I'm here for anything the costume team want to throw at me.'

'It's a great platform and for me personally, as a kid growing up, I never once imagined I would be doing any of this,' he says. 'Hopefully, the fact that people see me dancing a Rumba on Saturday-night telly will motivate others that look like me or sound like me to think, "If he can do it, I can do it."'

While he's a novice in the ballroom and Latin dances, Tyler is in no doubt that he's in it to win it.

'I would love to lift the glitterball,' he says. 'I would be my mum's favourite son for the rest of her life. Lifting the glitterball would be an amazing achievement and a dream come true. But either way, just stepping out on the dance floor in week one, I will feel like I have already won.'

Dianne Buswell

Australian

pro Dianne Buswell has teamed up with Kiss FM presenter Tyler West for series 20 and they already have a catchy team name – TyDi. Partnered on the London Eye, Dianne says she can't wait to take Tyler for a spin around the floor.

'Tyler didn't think he would be paired with me, so when he saw me he fell to the floor in pure shock,' she says. 'I hope it was a good shock!

'I am so happy to be paired with Tyler. He has a lot of energy, which is amazing, and so much potential. I'm really excited to see how much he can bring to the table – and to the dance floor.'

As a DJ and radio presenter, Tyler has an ear for music and Dianne is hoping that will translate to his feet.

'Rhythm and musicality is a massive strength and a big help when it comes to intricate timings,' she says. 'It's so nice as a choreographer to work with that, and having a partner who understands that is a huge, huge plus.

'Tyler is juggling work and training, but he really wants to do this and when he's in the rehearsal room he's really committed and giving it 100 per cent,' she says. 'I can't ask for any more than that. The main thing is that our personalities clicked straight away and we are genuinely having a great time so the time just flies by.'

The pair are kicking off with an American Smooth and, Dianne thinks he has made an impressive start.

'We have worked a lot on his ballroom frame and that is coming along really nicely,' she says. 'I think he's got a nice soft side to him as much as the spicy Latin skills, so an all-rounder is what I'm aiming for.'

Born in Western Australia, Dianne partnered brother Andrew from a young age. She became Australian Open Champion and four-time Amateur Australian Open Finalist, before joining the Australian version of *Strictly Come Dancing*. She joined the UK series in 2017 and, the following year, she reached the Final with social media star Joe Sugg. Last year, she partnered comedian Robert Webb, but he had to drop out of the competition in week three for health reasons.

'As short as it was, we had a really good time and Robert was great fun,' she says. 'Robert was really enjoying it and had done an awesome Tango and a Quickstep, but obviously his health is much more important. I look back on the time we had with really fond memories.'

Looking over her competition this year, Dianne thinks the viewers are in for a treat.

'This is a very strong batch of celebrities and they all seem lovely,' she says. 'I think there are some pretty good dancers and a lot of dark horses.'

As she kicks off her season with Tyler, Dianne is hoping to make it to the Final but is also setting a few benchmarks along the way.

'I would love to do Musicals Week again because I've only done that once,' she says. 'I really want to get to Blackpool because, as a dancer growing up, it was my dream to compete there. The first time I actually danced there was with Joe, which was so special, and I felt like I had finally fulfilled my childhood dreams. It would be really cool to dance there again.

'I've got high hopes for TyDi and obviously we want to go as far as we can. But the main thing I really want to focus on is Tyler having a good time, as I think that shines through in the dance.'

Anton Du Beke

As an integral part of the show from the first episode, Anton Du Beke is going into his twentieth series as one of three *Strictly* originals – alongside Craig Revel Horwood and Tess Daly. And he's delighted to be back on the judges' panel for the second year running.

'Being part of the best show on television, for 20 series, is remarkable,' he says. 'Craig, Tess and I are the longest-serving people on *Strictly* in the world because the UK *Strictly* has been going longer than the shows in America, or anywhere else. It's a massive honour and I feel very proud to be part of it.'

First paired with Lesley Garrett in 2004, Anton has danced some of *Strictly*'s most memorable routines throughout his time as a professional, twirling with the likes of Ann Widdecombe, Jerry Hall, Judy Murray and Nancy Dell'Olio. Last year, he shifted seamlessly from pro to judge, using his own experience of the competition to offer sage advice to the celebrity contestants.

'I enjoyed it enormously,' he says. 'I was thrilled to be on the panel, and I thought the series was amazing. I'm thrilled to be back, but then I'm always thrilled to be part of *Strictly Come Dancing*.'

While he loves his new role, Anton admits there were one or two moments in the last series when he missed being on the floor – but there's one aspect of competing he gladly dodged.

'I got a bit of dance envy with some of the numbers, wishing I could have done them, but that left me during the results show, knowing I would have been standing there waiting to hear if I was eliminated,' he says. 'The worst thing about *Strictly* is getting voted off, so I'm pleased I don't have to go through that anymore!'

Although Anton is reserving judgement on the dancing skills until the couples take to the floor in week one, he says the line-up has the makings of another memorable series.

'The 2022 cast are super, a great bunch, so it's going to be an exciting year,' he says. 'I'm looking forward to getting the audience back in.'

He is also delighted to be returning to Blackpool and says dancing at the Tower Ballroom is something all the couples want to achieve.

'It's a lovely moment in the series when we all get up and go to Blackpool and the show is bigger, brighter, louder, with extra dancers, more audience members – and all in that wonderful ballroom. It punctuates the series and I always used to tell my celebrity partner, "If you get to Blackpool, you've had a good run." After Blackpool, it's a push to the Final and the favourites come to the fore so it suddenly gets serious, but there's something so special about dancing in the Tower Ballroom.'

Another unforgettable moment came last year, when current champ Rose danced her moving Couple's Choice, which Anton called *Strictly*'s 'greatest dance ever'.

'Rose and Giovanni's Couple's Choice was so poignant; it became iconic almost immediately. It was just a special moment. But they did so many beautiful routines and Rose was remarkable.'

This year, Anton says viewers can expect surprises, twists and turns along the way, and he believes the audience vote means the Final is always going to be a thriller.

'The great thing about the *Strictly* Final is that it's judged by the audience, who I call the fifth judge and most important judge,' he says. 'The audience having the casting vote gives it the elevation and gravitas it needs, as well as all the unexpected twists. They always choose a great winner.'

As he celebrates the landmark show this year, Anton reveals how it has grown over the years, since the first show in 2004.

'*Strictly*'s lasting appeal is that it keeps evolving. It's been a gradual change, but the family remains together. The viewers are part of the show, which I think is integral to its success, and it's family viewing, which is important. It's a brilliant show and long may it continue.'

Lauren Oakley

New pro Lauren Oakley was born into the world of Latin and ballroom – almost literally. Although she officially started dancing at the age of two, she had an even earlier experience on the competition circuit.

'My mum, Jacquie, is a professional ballroom and Latin dancer and she won the British National when she was pregnant with me!' she reveals. 'So I started really young.'

Born and raised in Birmingham, Lauren was competing from the age of seven and was winning world championships from the age of nine. She is two-time UK Under-21 Latin Champion, British Under-21 Latin Champion and UK and British Under-21 Ballroom Champion. A huge fan of *Strictly*, Lauren says she is still pinching herself after becoming one of four new recruits in the pro team.

'I can't believe it's happening,' she says. 'I've grown up watching the show since the year it started and it's always been a dream of mine. So it's a mixture of being shocked, surprised and overwhelmed, but also feeling that this is the next natural step in my career, and what I've been leading up to.'

Lauren was visiting her grandmother in Birmingham when she took the call confirming her place on the show. 'I didn't know what to say because I was completely speechless!' she laughs. 'I did cry a bit as well, but in a good way. My nan was over the moon because she loves the show.'

Lauren loves both ballroom and Latin and says her favourite dance 'changes day by day'.

'If I'm in a happy mood, I love the Jive or the Quickstep, and if I'm feeling emotional, I love the Foxtrot or the Rumba. If I had to choose, I'd say the Rumba because it gives me the opportunity to do the most storytelling of all of the dances. It can be a love story or a break-up story, so happiness or heartbreak.'

Growing up in the ballroom and Latin world, Lauren remembers the first series of *Strictly* and says it helped change perceptions of the dance styles.

'The show has done so much for the ballroom and Latin world because, before *Strictly*, it had a reputation of being something for an older generation, at a social dance,' she says. '*Strictly* has brought it into people's living rooms and shown the magic of two people dancing together, how cool it can be and how you can apply it to any music. It's also shown how a non-dancer can fall in love with it, lose their inhibitions and throw themselves into the sparkle of it all.

'I started dancing because of my mum, before *Strictly* began, but having it on the TV every weekend helped me at school, because the kids knew what it was about and I didn't have to explain. They just got it.'

Having competed at Blackpool numerous times as a child, Lauren is looking forward to returning as part of the *Strictly* team.

'As a dancer competing in Blackpool, every time you step into the ballroom, it brings back different emotions like nerves, excitement and just how magical it is in there. It means a lot to ballroom and Latin dancers and I can't wait to dance there again.'

Lauren is also looking forward to taking part in the amazing pro dances on the weekend shows.

'I think the pro dances are absolutely incredible. There are fabulous concepts, the music is amazing and when you're dancing to the live band, it fills you with energy and gives you a real buzz. Also, I can't wait to experience the excitement of the live shows because I know what it means to sit in on a Saturday night with your family and watch *Strictly*. Being a part of it on the other side will be incredible.'

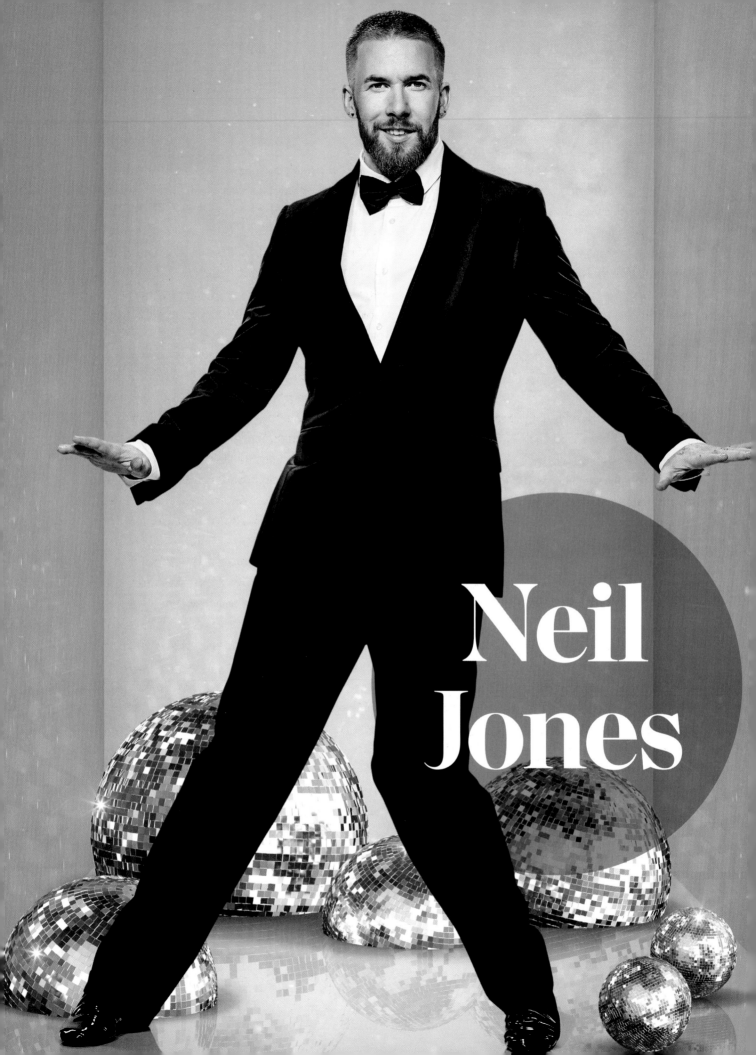

Neil
Jones

Neil

Jones is excited to see the latest celebrities take to the floor. And he says this year's partnerships are a recipe for success.

'The launch show was brilliant and the new celebrities look great,' he says. 'There's so much energy from them and so many different personalities. I'm loving the partnerships – they all seem perfect. We've already put together some incredible group numbers and I'm always excited for the music acts each week. It feels like it's going to be another great year.'

Neil is looking forward to watching the couples as they embark on their *Strictly* journey, and he has some sage advice for them.

'Every year, I love how you fall in love with certain couples, seeing what they go through and how invested they get in the whole experience,' he says. 'I've been speaking to a few of them, sharing that the most important thing is to fully invest in every single part of the show. Let go and let *Strictly* take over.'

Born in Münster, Germany, where his army dad was stationed, Neil started dancing at the age of three and trained in ballet, tap, modern, ballroom and Latin. He represented Finland, the Netherlands and the UK in his competitive career and holds 45 dance championship titles, including eight-time British National, eight-time Dutch National, European and four-time World Latin Champion. Joining *Strictly Come Dancing* in 2016, Neil partnered comedian Nina Wadia in series 19, but sadly they were the first to be eliminated.

'Nina was great. I really enjoyed the two dances we did, especially the Samba. I loved how she shocked everyone, because people weren't expecting that Samba from her. I thought that was brilliant and I will always remember that dance.

'Nina worked hard in training and we had a similar sense of humour, so we had a lot of fun too.'

Neil also took part in the Christmas special, getting a perfect score for his Street/Commercial dance to 'Ice Ice Baby' with comedian Mel Giedroyc.

'That was my first ever perfect score on *Strictly*!' he says. 'I hope one day in the future I can do the full series with Mel. She was a brilliant student, lovely to be around, so enthusiastic and a massive fan of the show.'

Since then, Neil has had a busy year, starring in the *Strictly Come Dancing Live!* tour, the *Strictly Come Dancing: The Professionals* tour and the live theatre tour, *Strictly Presents: Keeeep Dancing!*

'It was so nice to be performing to a live audience again, and the *Strictly* fans are amazing. They watch all their favourites on TV week in and week out and this is a chance to see them live. It was brilliant to see how much they enjoyed it.'

As one of the most experienced dancers on the team, Neil has welcomed the four new professionals and says he is on hand to offer any help and guidance they might want.

'They're settling in great,' he says. 'I've worked with Michelle Tsiakkas and she's a brilliant dancer, and I know Lauren Oakley from when she was competing, and she is very talented. Lauren and I will be dancing together for one of the first music acts, so I'm looking forward to that. Vito Coppola has already done the show in Italy, so even though it's different, he knows what he's in for. Carlos Gu, who I've known for years, has a massive personality and I think the British public are going to love him.

'It's exciting and they're all going to be great, so my only advice is to enjoy it. But I don't feel like they need any advice. They're incredible!'

Neil says the lasting appeal of the show is the happiness it brings to fans.

'I think it's escapism. It's entertaining, but viewers are getting real life in there as well,' he says. 'More than that, it's a positive, happy place to be.'

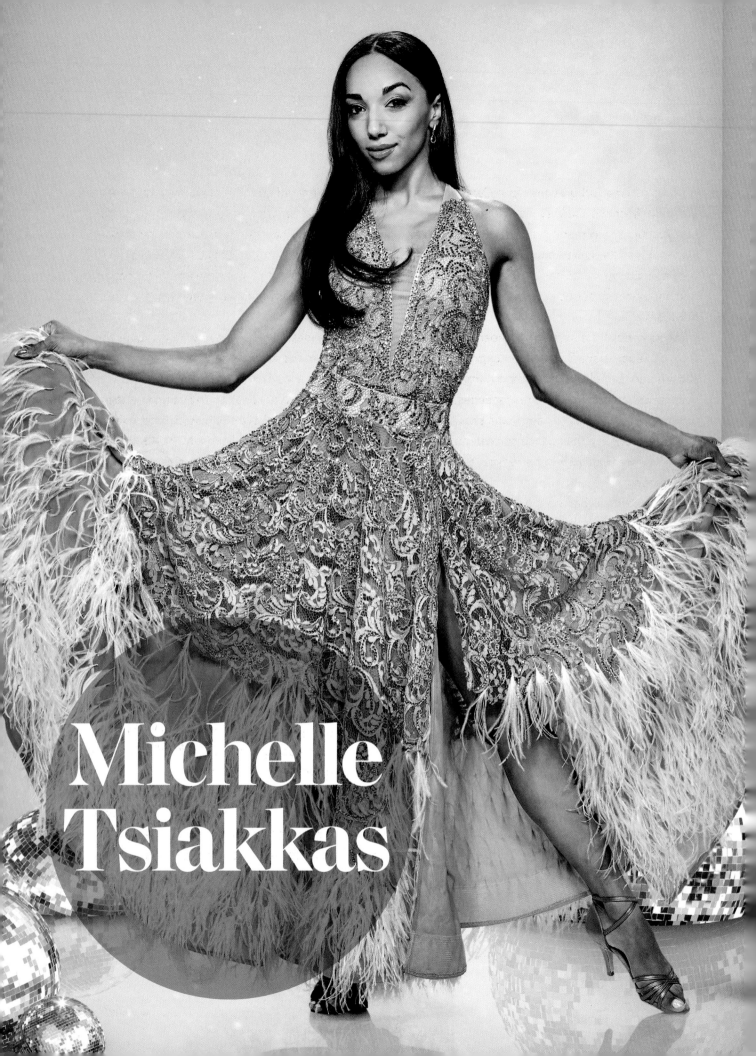

Michelle Tsiakkas

As a little girl growing up in Cyprus, Michelle Tsiakkas was glued to *Strictly* every Saturday night and dreamed of taking her own place on the hallowed dance floor. Now the Latin champ's wish has been granted as she becomes one of four new recruits to join the pro team.

'I'm so happy,' she says. 'It's a dream come true. A lot of people have British TV in Cyprus and the show is very popular, so I watched it from a very young age, probably since the first series. It's always been my dream to be on the show. When it finally happened, it was such a surreal moment.'

Michelle was just six when she first fell in love with dance.

'I tried Latin and ballroom and I knew just from my first dance class that it was the thing for me. I felt so happy after my first lesson, I wanted to go back and do it again. Over the years, the passion got stronger and stronger.'

Competing from the age of six, the talented dancer became Cypriot National Champion for 10 consecutive years. At 16, Michelle took a break from competing to study architecture at the University of Kent, in Canterbury, where she continued to dance as a hobby.

'I am passionate about architecture so I wanted both the dancing and the academic career,' she says. 'But my passion for dancing was so strong and there came a point that I had to tell myself, "If you want to dance, you need to take the plunge. Are you going to take that risk?" I needed to try even if I failed because I didn't want to have any regrets. I'm so happy I made that decision now.'

In 2019, Michelle returned to dance full-time, turning professional and competing for the UK at major competitions before she got the call from *Strictly Come Dancing*.

'I was in Italy when they called me and it was so emotional, I started crying,' she says. 'I don't think it sank in that I really am part of the show until the launch show, but once I was there, with the cameras, the audience and the amazing atmosphere, it felt so much more real. It's incredible.'

Michelle wasn't the only one who was over the moon about her new role.

'My family are so excited for me,' she says. 'My mum is so emotional. I think when she sees me dance on the first show, she'll be crying a lot.'

Although she loves ballroom, Michelle says she's 'more of a Latin girl', and Samba is her favourite dance.

'Latin comes to me more naturally because the fiery, passionate, side is more me,' she says. 'I love the Samba because I love the rhythm of samba music, I love the motions of the dance because it's all in the hips. Having said that, ballroom is a beautiful dance style and it's great dancing ballroom as a couple because you move as one.'

Michelle met the pro team at rehearsals for the group dances this summer, and she says they were 'all really lovely and made me feel very comfortable straight away'.

Now a fully-fledged part of the *Strictly* family, Michelle says being in the studio for the live show is even more magical than she'd hoped.

'Watching at home as a child, all you see is magic,' she says. 'You look at the pros, think they're the best dancers in the world, so you want to be there. Now I can say that being in it, there's even more magic. Everyone on the show is so good at what they do and I'm just in awe of everyone, from the make-up, wardrobe, the staging, choreographers, dancers – everybody is at the top of their game. It's just such a magical show.'

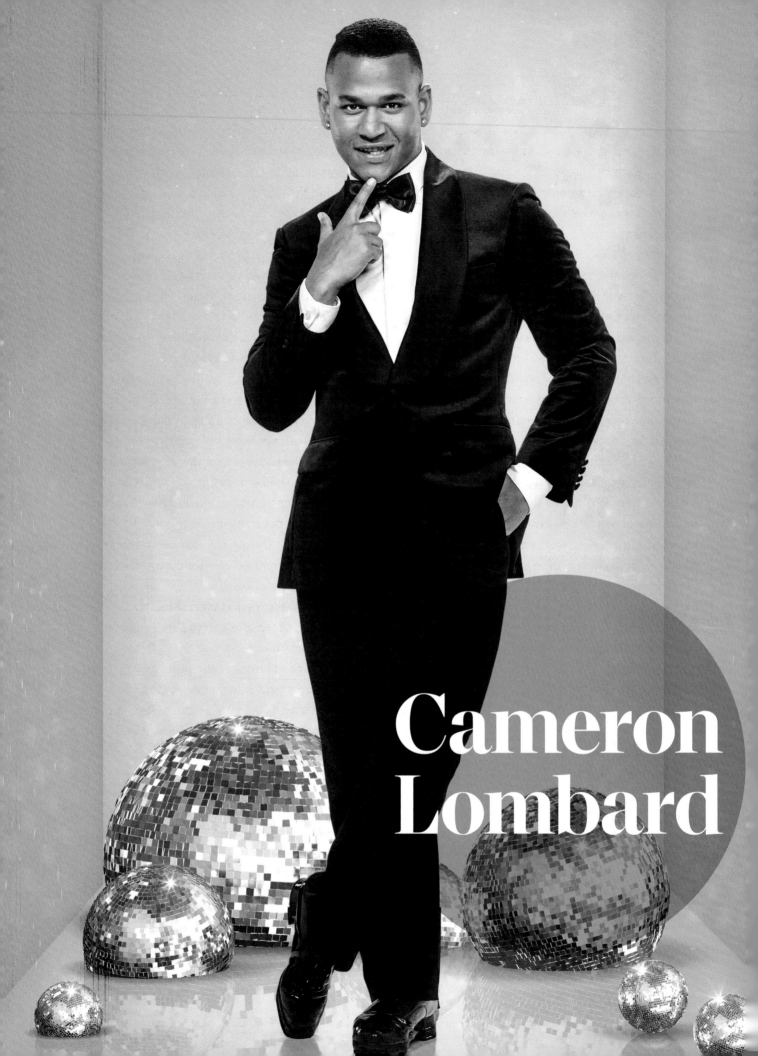

Cameron
Lombard

Cameron Lombard returns for his second stint on *Strictly* and he is excited to be part of the pro team once again. The South African dancer says he has already had an unforgettable moment, at the launch show, when he danced for one of his musical heroes.

'The launch show was absolutely amazing and I got to perform with John Legend, who was singing his new release,' he says. 'That was a big thing for me and it was a really fun start to the new series. I think this will be a special year. There's a really good competition ahead and the new group of celebrities has some really talented people, but they are all really lovely and easy to talk to.

'The group dances are also going to be spectacular this year, embracing some different styles and different cultures of dance. So I'm expecting a great series.'

Born in Cape Town, Cameron began dancing at the age of five after catching the bug while watching his older sister compete. He went on to become South African National Champion, winning 18 national titles across ballroom and Latin. In 2012, he was a finalist on *South Africa's Got Talent* and in 2019 he represented his country at the World Championships. Last year was his *Strictly* debut and he says the highlight, for him, was the moment before he stepped onto the floor for the first time.

'My first year on *Strictly* was mind-blowing for me and my family,' he says. 'The stand-out memory was my debut performance, with Anne-Marie as the music act. Particularly the moment just before it happened, when the judges, professionals and the *Strictly* fans were about to see me dance for the first time. Just entering the *Strictly* ballroom, and performing with Anne-Marie, was such a privilege.'

As well as dancing on the main show, Cameron toured with the *Strictly Come Dancing Live!*, Strictly *Come Dancing: The Professionals* and the *Strictly Presents* tour, which were brand-new experiences for him.

'I was able to see so many *Strictly* fans that love the show and people whose lives have been changed by it, and to see what life it brings to their faces was amazing. Performing in each different city, seeing how happy we make the fans, lifted my performance because you knew people were going back to their homes feeling happy, because of what we do.

'It was the first time I've performed for so many people, and it was amazing to see different types of theatres and find out about the history of each place. I've learned a lot. I've seen a lot and I'm so grateful to be a part of the show still.'

The youngest pro on the team, Cameron says he is still learning all he can from his fellow dancers.

'This year, I'm looking forward to gaining more experience,' he says. 'I'm still learning from the other professionals, learning more about communicating with the celebrities and being able to teach them to dance while having fun, and eventually I can put that into my own work.'

Cameron says he grew up with the show and was inspired by fellow South Africans Johannes Radebe and Oti Mabuse.

'I started dancing very young and I always knew about *Strictly*, but I never thought I'd be able to be a part of it,' he says. 'But watching from home and seeing Johannes and Oti on the show, I was wishing and wondering if that could one day be me, so that's what I worked toward. When I got the call, I was so grateful to be able to share the same stage with them, representing South Africa. Being part of the original *Strictly* show is a complete dream come true.

'The show puts smiles on everybody's faces and it has a real impact on lives, not just in the UK, but all around the world. It's about hoping and making dreams a reality – making the impossible possible. In the same way, I once thought it was impossible for me to be on *Strictly*, but it became possible. That's something I'll cherish for the rest of my life.'

Luba
Mushtuk

Returning

for her fifth year as a *Strictly* pro, Luba Mushtuk is excited about the new group of celebrities heading for the dance floor and says viewers are in for a treat.

'It's going to be beautiful, big and, as always, very entertaining,' she says. 'I think it's a great bunch of celebrities. The first time they danced together, at the launch show, it was fantastic. They are all so nice and down to earth, which is important. I spotted quite a few who have potential and I think there will be some surprises this year.'

Luba was born in St Petersburg but moved to Italy aged 12 to study dance under legendary teacher Catarina Arzenton, becoming four-time winner of the Italian Dance Championship and Italian Open Latin Show Dance Champion. Growing up as a competitor, she has fond memories of Blackpool and says she always looks forward to dancing there with her fellow pros.

'Blackpool has its own atmosphere, its own energy,' she says. 'It always feels very special to dance there, for me, personally, because I danced at the Tower Ballroom when I was a kid. It was always the event of the year and nothing compared to it, so I'm really looking forward to that.'

Luba is thrilled to be dancing the group numbers and has one particular favourite this year.

'Every year *Strictly* goes up another level and the pro dances get better and better.'

Luba will also be taking the floor during the live sets from the incredible musical acts who appear on the results show. But she admits launch-show guest John Legend left her a little starstruck.

'The John Legend dance was very special,' she says. 'I'm a huge fan and have been to his concerts so it was incredible to meet him. He was so kind and very welcoming, talking to us as if he knew us already, and when he performs he's such an incredible artist. It was a beautiful moment.'

Since joining *Strictly* in 2018, Luba has partnered Olympian James Cracknell and American football star Jason Bell, and she has some sage advice for the incoming celebrities.

'I would tell them to listen to their professional partner at all times. All of our *Strictly* professionals are such amazing teachers and they know what to do, how to do it and when to do it. So trust the process and completely trust in your professional partner.'

Welcoming the four new pros to the show, Luba says they have already settled in and 'feel like they've been there forever'.

'They are all lovely and each one brings something different to the show,' she says. 'If I had to give them advice I would say simply adapt, absorb and learn.'

Last year Luba danced a Jive with Jay Blades to the iconic *Only Fools and Horses* theme on the Christmas special.

'It was fun, because I did some cultural research by watching *Only Fools and Horses*,' she says. 'It's so iconic in the UK and everybody knows about it, but I had never seen it. But Jay was amazing. He's very clever, deep and profound, and it was a pleasure to spend time with him.'

Since then Luba has been busy, on the *Strictly Come Dancing Live!* arena tour and dancing with her fellow pro dancers on *Strictly Come Dancing: The Professionals* theatre tour.

'The arena tour was amazing and great fun, and the pro tour was fantastic,' she says. 'The company was amazing; we had so much fun and we were so excited for the show itself that two hours flew by every night.'

Now buzzing to be back in the studio, Luba says the beauty of the show is that there's 'something for everyone'.

'It's the best show on television and everyone can relate to it,' she says. 'People can be inspired by it. Families with kids watch it together. It's a beautiful, joyful show that makes you forget your troubles and just enjoy being entertained.'

Answers

Word Search

C	B	A	E	S	M	G	R	I	O	I	N	K	B
H									O	R	C	L	
R	J	O	L	L	C	E	K						
E	G	D	S	A	N	C		H	D	M		O	
V	U	S				F	R	O	Y	X		P	
Q	W	A	D		F	R	O	Y	X			O	
K	S		N	L	L			Z				C	
E	X	O	Y	X	V			N				L	
J	E	T	A									O	
L	T	Z		Y			X				P		
A	L	W		A	V		Z		O	E			
O													
Y	O	R	A	G	E	X	S	H	I		L	Y	A
I	J	V	I	E	N	E	W	Y	C	R	P	P	X
D	U	B	E								R	C	

CrossWord

1 K	E	L	V	I	N	■	3 G	4 G	A	R	R	5 A	W	6 A	Y
A		I			7 C	M	E			5 I		A		
8 T	A	N	G	9 O		A	E		10 L	A	T	I	N		11 N
E		D		W		M	R	E		E			E		I
	12 R	Y	A	N		E	I		Y		R		G
13 F		H			R		C					H
14 L	O	O	K		15 L	O	G	A	N		16 W	17 H	A	T
E		P			N		N			A		A
18 T	E	S	S		19 F	L	O	S	S		20 R	U	N
C					O		M		R		D
H		21 S		22 P	M		O		23 F	A	Y	E
E		A		I	B		O		A		J		24 B
25 R	U	M	B	A		26 A	N	T	O	N		27 U	G	O
	B		N		R		H			D		S
28 D	I	A	M	O	N	D	S	■	29 S	L	I	D	E	S

Answers

Quiz

1. 'The Show Must Go On' – Queen
2. Lesley Garrett
3. Charleston
4. *EastEnders* (Jill Halfpenny, Kara Tointon and Rose Ayling-Ellis)
5. Rose Ayling-Ellis and Giovanni Pernice
6. Anne-Marie
7. Lobster
8. South Africa
9. Cruella de Vil
10. Tom Fletcher and Amy Dowden
11. Louise Redknapp and Danny Mac
12. Jill Halfpenny
13. Karen Hauer
14. Blackpool Tower Ballroom
15. Quentin Willson

Guess the Dance

1. Charleston
2. Jive
3. Samba
4. Salsa
5. Quickstep
6. Argentine Tango
7. American Smooth
8. Paso Doble